D1483361

CONTEMPORARY STUDIES IN ECONOMIC AND FINANCIAL ANALYSIS

An International Series of Monographs

Implications of Regulation on Bank Expansion:
A Simulation Analysis

by GEORGE S. OLDFIELD, JR.
Graduate School of Business
and Public Administration
Cornell University

 JAI PRESS INC.

Greenwich, Connecticut

Library of Congress Cataloging in Publication Data

Oldfield, George S
  Implications of regulation on bank expansion.

  (Contemporary studies in economic and financial
analysis; v. 10)
    Bibliography: p.
    Includes index.
    1. Banks and banking—United States—Mathematical
models. 2. Banks and banking—United States—State
supervision—Mathematical models.   I. Title. II. Series.
HG1586.053   332.1'6'0973   76-10399
ISBN 0-89232-015-X

Contents

Tables

Chapter I

Introduction

A complicated system of rules prevents commercial banks from freely branching and merging in the United States. While the initiative for expansion rests with individual banks, two separate types of growth constraints are used by state and federal governments. First, state banking law defines the organizational and geographic arrangements that are permissable for banks in the state. For example, a state law might allow banks to branch and merge throughout the state, but disallow the formation of multiple bank holding companies. Second, as banks propose various branch locations and mergers allowed by state law, federal regulatory agencies and the courts respond with case-by-case decisions about the rules governing expansion. No well defined regulatory guidelines exist.

The evolution of a state's banking industry may be strongly influenced by laws and regulations. However, almost nothing is known about the impact of these rules on the provision of local banking services. Typically, the long run consequences of each new office or acquisition can be discerned only vaguely. The competitive effect of a bank's proposal may appear slight at first. As a pattern

1

of expansion emerges though, the eventual consequences of earlier precedents might produce anticompetitive results. Since the effects of ad hoc regulatory and legal decisions are presently unpredictable, the cumulative impact of apparently sound individual decisions may be contrary to actual policy objectives.

This study starts with the existing federal and state banking structure control apparatus as a frame of reference. Within this institutional setting, several important issues are investigated. First, it is important to decompose the interactions between external control procedures and the natural expansion behavior of banks. This is essential for analyzing the unique impacts of alternative regulatory policies and state laws. Second, it is important to discover whether different control instruments have a significant impact on banking structure. If there is no measurable influence generated by alternative laws and policies the selection of specific instruments is a matter of indifference. Conversely, if some laws and policies create significantly different banking structures, then it is crucial to choose proper instruments. This introduces the third issue. A comprehensive choice procedure is developed to demonstrate how preferred laws and policies can be identified.

A monte carlo simulation procedure is used to create sequences of hypothetical bank expansions that result from the combined effects of innate bank behavior and the constraints imposed by regulation. This technique allows experimental trials of several different policy alternatives once a mathematical description of the banking environment is specified. The simulation model rests on the proposition that banks branch, merge, and form holding companies in a predictable manner to exploit the legal and regulatory options available. For example, if a state's banking law allows statewide branching, certain types of banks extend branch networks across the entire state. Given this framework, a heuristic model incorporating observed external characteristics of merging, branching, and holding company behavior is employed rather than a rigorous microeconomic theory of bank operations. Consequently, optimal structure issues are not considered in a microeconomic sense of efficiency. The primary objective is to explore the eventual competitive implications of various legislative and regulatory alternatives interacting with innate bank behavior. Policymakers can then choose instruments that generate preferred competitive outcomes.

Banking structure change is determined in the simulation through the interaction of three influences. First, bank behavior provides the motive force for the external expansion activity that produces changes in market structure. Within the simulation, equations estimated from observed expansion behavior govern the stochastic merger and de novo (new) branching processes. Federal regulatory policy is a second factor that influences banking structure change. In the following analysis, three distinct regulatory policies are constructed and their competitive consequences separately examined. The final factor influencing banking structure change in the simulation is state law. Four alternative state laws are defined and tested below. Each is modeled as a group of deterministic operating rules that constrains banks' expansion choice sets.

The federal agencies that directly exercise control over banking structure are assumed to implement a uniform regulatory policy. Actually, the United States Department of Justice acts as a screen above the Federal Reserve System, the Federal Deposit Insurance Corporation, and the United States Comptroller of the Currency to assure consistency in policy application. In the three different regulatory rules specified for the study, no distinction is made among the agencies. The focus of the separate policies is different enough so that the impact of federal oversight can be analyzed.

State banking law comprises a separate set of rules that is known completely to a state's commercial banks prior to any expansion attempt. The four laws analyzed are similar to those currently existing in various states. The laws cover a range of expansion control from fairly restrictive to little constraint. For each law, all three regulatory policies are tested independently. This procedure is repeated separately for the four different laws, creating twelve separate regulatory-legal combinations. The twelve pairings of banking law and regulatory policy cover the possibilities from lenient policy matched with unrestrictive law to a combination of quite stringent law and policy.

The experimental framework for the study is the 1971 commercial banking structure in Pennsylvania, a useful starting point for three reasons. First, there were a large number of banks and banking offices in the state. Second, the state law governing expansion allowed enough branching and merging in the 1960s so that a wide range of bank behavior was manifest. Finally, the 1970 census data allowed the study to begin with a contemporaneous body of demographic data. Thus, one state's actual banking industry is the closed system used for testing the effects of laws and regulations on the evolution of local banking competition.

A single simulation experiment is conducted by specifying sets of decision rules that denote a particular regulatory policy and state law. The availability of three different regulatory policies and four separate state laws creates twelve possible experimental combinations of control instruments. However, the rules governing innate bank behavior remain invariant across all twelve control instrument combinations.[1] In this fashion, the unique influence on market structure of each regulatory-legal alternative can be contrasted. In addition, each experiment is repeated several times with an identical parameterization to generate frequency distributions of quantitative market structure measures. These distributions are analyzed to yield information concerning the relative performance of each law and regulatory policy. An experiment conducted with the presently operable state law and regulatory policy provides a control solution against which the structural impacts of alternative instruments can be gauged.

The following study is separated into eight sections. Chapter II consists of a review of recent literature relevant to bank expansion simulation. Chapter III presents the rationale for using a monte carlo simulation to investigate the merging and de novo branching processes. In addition, the major assumptions of the analysis and the general operation of the model are detailed. The definitions of the four hypothetical laws investigated in the simulation are contained in Chapter IV. In Chapter V, a quantitative analysis of bank merger regulation is presented. A statistical analysis of legal decisions concerning bank mergers provides decision rules for the regulatory segment of the simulation. Research into bank behavior is contained in Chapter VI. The assumptions, methodology, and results for estimating the relationships which govern the model's merger and de novo branch procedures are detailed here. Chapter VII presents the outcomes of experiments with various state laws and regulatory policies. Several measures of concentration and service availability are used to quantify the impact of bank expansion control instruments at both the statewide and local levels. A unified framework for regulatory and legislative decision making is detailed in Chapter VIII. The analysis addresses the problems of aggregating local results and choosing among instruments that have an uncertain impact on target variables. The final chapter is a summary.

NOTES
1. With the exception of some learning behavior described in Chapter V.

Chapter II

Review of Recent Research in Commercial Banking Organization

Analysis of various organizational and operational aspects of the commercial banking industry has attracted considerable research effort in the past several years. Two related factors contribute to this interest. The commercial banking system occupies a central position among financial intermediaries as the government's agent for managing currency transactions and transmitting economic policy. As a direct consequence, few industries are more heavily regulated. A salient feature of this regulation is the pervasive influence exercised at both state and federal levels over commercial banks' organization and market structure. The primary objective of this regulation is to promote a competitive, secure, and publicly convenient money and credit distribution system. Economic analyses of organization costs, expansion motives, and industry evolution seek to create a better understanding of the commercial banking system's operation and to improve the implementation of structural control policies.

A brief review of some recent research in commercial banking provides a background for the current study. Such a survey is necessary to indicate the relevant considerations in modeling the bank merger and de novo branching processes for use in this study.

7

In general, the results cited suggest that expansion motives do not derive from observable operating cost economies. In addition, previous studies of bank expansion have not extensively considered such important issues as the interactions of mergers and branches in local market structure and the combined impacts of legal and regulatory control instruments. Therefore, the analyses summarized in this chapter provide a preliminary basis for the simulation .

ECONOMETRIC COST STUDIES
OF MULTIPLE BRANCH BANKING

Extensive research has been directed toward investigating possible cost motivations for observed multiple office expansion activity. These studies could have considerable potential value for an industry expansion model if direct operating benefits and optimal branch bank size could be identified. The econometric cost studies are based upon rigorous theoretical models of internal bank operations and employ both single function and multiple function output measures.[1] In the single function method, output is measured as a weighted index of various commercial bank activities (demand deposits, consumer loans, etc.). The multiple function approach treats each separate activity as producing an independent output. Given the output measure used, a reduced form cost equation derived from a specific production function (usually Cobb-Douglas) is estimated from cross-section data.

Two alternative experimental designs are advocated in the literature for relating operating costs to market structure. Arguments for each derive from optimal banking structure considerations and the identification of a least cost banking industry composition. In the first method, branch banks and unit banks of the same size (however measured in terms of output) are compared.[2] The implicit assumption is that an equal number of firms will exist in an industry independent of legally available organizational structures. The second approach compares branch banks with equal size aggregations of unit banks.[3] For example, the cost of operating five unit banks is compared with the cost of operating one branch bank with five offices. This construct's implicit assumption is that an equal number of banking offices will operate in an industry independent of organizational alternatives.

The results of extensive econometric cost analyses are not unanimous but most recent work indicates the following.[4] First, regardless of output measure or experimental design, unit banks appear to be less costly organizations than branch banks on the basis of direct operating costs. Second, banks larger than $5 to $10 million in deposits do not generally realize substantial economies of scale in producing banking services and also display diseconomies in branching. Finally, branching diseconomies appear to decrease as the number of branches increases. However, operating cost analyses may fail to account fully for an important factor underlying multiple office operations. It is likely that branch banking internalizes some of the transportation cost that customers incur when utilizing bank services. Thus the additional cost of multiple branch banking should be considered a convenience or service return paid indirectly to customers rather than a surplus operating cost. Analyses confined to narrowly defined measures of cost do not adequately value this phenomenon.[5]

Another related rationale for branching may derive from price discrimination considerations. A bank can attract business from a locale either by making its rates on deposits and loans more attractive at existing facilities or by opening an office at the locale. If rate alterations are attempted, all of a bank's present customers benefit and competition may eliminate any price advantage in attracting new business. Conversely, a new office primarily serving the new locale may affect only the marginal new customers. Thus the cost of a new branch strategy may be far less than a price competition attempt. Operating cost studies overlook this possibility.

In summary, statistical cost analyses based upon precise theoretical models of banks' internal operations are generally directed toward identifying narrowly defined efficient organization designs and optimal banking structures. The results of these studies leave both the branching motivation and optimal structure issues unanswered because current models and data do not allow a complete specification of the problem.

MULTIVARIATE ANALYSES OF BANK BEHAVIOR

An alternative method for analyzing bank behavior focuses on the measured characteristics of banks' observed choices in a given decision situation. No direct optimization model is defined in these studies although variables relating to profitability are generally included. The mode of study splits banks' behavior into two or more mutually exclusive groups. For example, Gilbert examines bank branching activity following regulatory action on a proposed merger.[6] The objective is to define a function that discriminates between two discrete groups. The first group contains banks that opened a de novo branch in the same market area where they had recently attempted a merger. The regulatory decision on the merger may have been either affirmative or negative. The second group contains banks that did not open a de novo branch following the regulatory decision.

A large group of variables is defined to describe the attributes of the decision situation. For example, variables such as total assets, number of offices recently opened, and total mergers initiated are measured for each bank in both groups. In addition, economic variables like total retail sales, number of banks operating, and market concentration are used to describe the market area of the proposed merger. Then a function is estimated based upon the initiator bank and market variables that best divides the target banks into their proper groups. Gilbert's results show that a significant level of discriminating power is obtained by using variables that characterize the banks involved and the choice environment. Although each observation is ex post, it is assumed that the discriminant function is stationary and provides a proper classification tool for describing bank behavior.

Based upon Gilbert's work, it is apparent that discriminant techniques provide a useful method for analyzing banks' choices in discrete decision situations. This is particularly true where a natural classification of behavior is possible. For example, branch/no branch outcomes are truly mutually exclusive outcomes at a certain decision point. Other uses of discriminant analysis to separate banks into groups may encounter problems if the class definitions are artificial. For example, Sinkey investigates whether financial ratios can be used to discriminate between problem banks and sound banks.[7] The ex post groupings are based upon arbitrary bank examination criteria. In this case, it is not clear that banks defined in either group are actual group members except in examiners' minds. An extensive discussion of such problems relating to the application of discriminant analysis is contained in a recent survey article by Eisenbeis.[8]

A MARKOV MODEL OF BANKING STRUCTURE EVOLUTION

Two alternative quantitative techniques have recently been proposed to investigate the effects of mergers on a state's banking industry structure. In one, Yeats employs a Markov transition model to forecast changes in three states' banking structures resulting from different regulatory policies.[9] The analysis abstracts from individual bank behavior entirely and treats structural change as a stable process at an aggregate statewide level. In an alternative approach Juncker and Oldfield utilize a monte carlo simulation model to analyze the impact of various combinations of bank behavior and regulatory policies on one state's local banking market structure.[10] Unlike Yeats' model, the Juncker and Oldfield study is based upon individual banks' expansion behavior. Thus, while both studies rely upon probabilistic modeling techniques, the modes of analysis are quite different.

The Yeats analysis investigates bank merger activity in California, New Jersey, and North Carolina. A separate Markov transition model is estimated for each state. The study's objective is to forecast and contrast each state's eventual equilibrium market structure under three different regulatory policy specifications. The first regulatory policy assumes a continuation of the criteria employed by regulatory agencies between 1961 and 1968. The second policy specification is a simple no merger rule. The third policy is a rule making acquisitions by a state's ten largest banks strictly illegal. Since an identical technique is employed for each state and the equilibrium outcomes are also similar, this discussion is limited to a description of the methodology used and the general results.

Following Yeats, the analysis proceeds by first dividing all of a state's banks into eleven discrete, mutually exclusive and exhaustive size classes based upon the total deposits of each bank. A state vector $(S)t$ depicting the percent of banks in each size class at time t can then be defined:

$$(S)t = (S_0, S_1, \ldots, S_{11})t.$$

Next a stochastic (11 by 11) transition matrix (P) is defined. The element (p_{ij}) of (P) represents the probability that a bank in the ith size class will evolve into size class j by the next time period. The (p_{ij}) are assumed to remain constant through time; in addition, $\sum\limits_{i} p_{ij} = \sum\limits_{j} p_{ij} = 1.00$.

A state vector and transition matrix can be utilized to project the next period's size distribution of banks through matrix multiplication:

$$(S)t + 1 = (S)t \cdot (P).$$

Moreover, given the constant (p_{ij}), n successive multiplications of (P) times $(S)t$ generate successive $(S)t + n$ state vectors depicting the size distribution of banks in period $t + n$. Sufficient successive multiplications (e) of $(S)t$ by (P) produce a steady state equilibrium where the elements of $(S)t + e$ are constant. That is, entries of banks into a given size class are exactly offset by exits from the size class. This represents the ultimate structural outcome of a particular merger policy.

An interesting aspect of this model involves size class 0. This represents the percentage of banks entering or exiting the banking industry. Similarly, row probabilities p_{oj} in (P) represent the probability of de novo entry into class j while column probabilities p_{jo} represent the probability of a jth class bank exiting the industry (usually through merger). A large pool of potential entrants is arbitrarily specified to assure the availability of new banks through time. By normalizing the $(S)t + 1$ vector such that $\sum\limits_{i=1}^{10} S_{it} + 1 = 1$, unbiased estimates of the percentage of banks in each size class are obtained. Thus the Markov transition model accounts for de novo entry into a state's banking industry.

Yeats independently estimates the model for North Carolina, New Jersey, and California. The estimation method is identical for each state. The initial state vector (S)t represents the size distribution of banks existing in 1961. The transition matrix (P) is constructed by measuring the actual transitions from 1961 to 1968. Since the (P) matrix is estimated from structural changes between 1961 and 1968, the transition probabilities are for a seven year period. That is, one multiplication of (S)1961 by (P) yields a 1968 banking structure and a second multiplication of (S)1961 by (P) creates (S)1975. This process eventually generates the steady state bank structure predicated upon the continuance of a stable 1961/68 regulatory policy.

To model the implications of a no merger policy Yeats estimates a merger adjusted transition matrix (P). The deposit sizes of banks existing in 1968 are corrected for mergers by subtracting from surviving banks any deposits (growth adjusted) acquired through merger. This yields a 1968 adjusted size distribution with which to estimate (P). The third regulatory policy, the "Top Ten" merger rule, utilizes a similar adjustment mechanism to correct for all mergers that involved the ten largest banks in the state.

The transition matrices are used to compute equilibrium bank size distributions resulting from alternative regulatory policies. To analyze the model's forecasts, Yeats uses the Gini ratio as a summary statistic to describe the steady state banking structure of each state.[11] The results demonstrate that, in terms of concentration of deposits at the statewide level, both the no merger rule and the "Top Ten" rule are superior to the rule employed by regulators during the 1961/68 period. Moreover, the "Top Ten" rule, a much more easily implemented policy, generates results not substantially inferior to the no merger rule. However, even a continuation of the historical policy creates lower Gini ratios in New Jersey and North Carolina and only marginally higher concentration in California when 1961 structure is compared to predicted equilibrium size distribution. Thus Yeats demonstrates that regulatory policy can have a considerable impact on statewide concentration and that fairly simple rules can generate substantial results.

A MONTE CARLO MODEL OF MERGER ACTIVITY

The Juncker and Oldfield paper employs a monte carlo simulation model of bank expansion activity in New Jersey to investigate several regulatory issues. The objectives of the analysis are to quantify the impact of various regulatory policies on the structure of local banking markets and to explore the relationship between bank behavior and regulatory policy. While the Yeats study is based upon transitions among classes of banks at a statewide level, the simulation deals with combinations of individual banks. Thus much more detailed results are obtained.

The simulation operates by repeatedly selecting a merger initiator, pairing the initiator with a feasible partner bank, and testing the hypothetical merger proposal against a regulatory policy. Merger activity is jointly controlled by three factors. First, assumptions concerning bank behavior determine an initiator's partner search activity. Second, an inflexible and invariable state law governs an initiator's feasible geographic merger areas. Third, regulatory policy probabilistically determines the types of mergers allowable. Four separate merger policies are tested. In addition, three general behavioral assumptions are tested in conjunction with regulatory policy. As in the Yeats analysis, the New Jersey bank expansion simulation groups all banks into mutually exclusive, discrete, and exhaustive classes. These classes are not strict size groupings; each class is assumed to represent a distinct behavior category. That is, it is assumed that all banks within a particular class display identical behavior while banks in different classes are dissimilar. While deposit size is the primary determinant of class membership, management quality and market share are also relevant. Behavior classes range from class I banks that represent potential statewide holding company lead banks to class V banks that are local, small unit banks.

The initial classification of each bank is accomplished through a case-by-case analysis of all New Jersey banks. In the simulation, simple rules reclassify surviving banks following acquisitions. For example, a class I bank combining with any class bank yields a class I bank; a class II bank combining with any class bank that results in aggregate deposits over $350 million yields a class I bank. Similar rules cover all class combinations. In this fashion, transitions between classes are simulated on an acquisition-by-acquisition basis as banks evolve in size and aggressiveness.

An acquisition attempt consists of selecting an initiator and matching it with an appropriate partner. Within the simulation, both decisions are governed by subjective class-specific probability densities. The initiation probabilities represent the authors' and their associates' best guesses of likely bank behavior based upon monitored bank expansion behavior in New Jersey. Initiation probabilities are assumed to remain constant for all banks of a given class relative to other class banks. For example, any class I bank always has twice the probability of initiating an acquisition attempt relative to any class II bank. As banks change classes, the initiation probabilities are adjusted to maintain the relative likelihoods of initiation. Conversely, partner selection probabilities may be varied. If initiators are assumed to search for partners with large total deposits, large bank preference behavior can be tested. Similarly, intermediate and small bank preference behaviors may be tested as alternative behavior patterns. In addition, fixed rules govern other aspects of partner selection. Initiators may not acquire banks larger than themselves. Also, class I and class II banks can search statewide for partners, class III and class IV banks are limited to districtwide search, and class V banks can acquire partners only in their own markets.

The banking law in New Jersey splits the state into three districts of roughly equal size. Holding companies are allowed to acquire subsidiaries statewide while mergers are allowed only within district boundaries. In addition, for purposes of competitive analysis, the Federal Reserve Bank of New York divides New Jersey into 19 local banking markets. These local markets are the basic units of analysis in the model. Note also that within the simulation, mergers and holding company acquisitions are identically treated and both are termed acquisitions.

Regulatory policy is specified in the model in a manner designed to parallel actual regulatory decision making. Based upon the behavior classes and markets of the initiator and partner, a proposed merger is categorized into one of seven judgment groups. Each group is assigned a probability of regulatory approval based upon the particular operative regulatory policy. The seven judgment groups with each regulatory policy's approval probability are displayed below.

Judgement groups	Regulatory Policies and Approval Probabilities			
	Restrictive	Moderate	Permissive	Very Liberal
Procompetitive	.99	.99	.99	.99
No adverse effects	.98	.99	.99	.99
Slightly adverse	.90	.98	.99	.99
Adverse	.25	.90	.98	.99
Substantially Adverse	.05	.25	.90	.98
Monopolistic	.02	.05	.25	.90
Monopoly	.01	.02	.05	.25

All bank class and market combinations are assigned to a specific judgment group. For example, a class III bank acquiring a class III bank in a different market might always be judged slightly adverse. Under the restrictive policy this combination has a .90 probability of approval while under the moderate policy it has a .98 probability of approval.

A simulation experiment is conducted by specifying a particular regulatory policy and size preference behavioral assumption. A run of 80 approved combinations is generated with the deposit size and office location data of the surviving bank updated after each combination. Since acquisition initiator selection, partner choice, and regulatory decisions are all stochastic, no two runs of the same experiment yield identical structural results. However, replication of an experiment produces frequency distributions of objective competitive measures that may be compared among experiments.

The Juncker and Oldfield study analyzes three general sets of results, each at both a statewide level and within six selected local markets. Statewide outcomes are measured with a ten-bank concentration ratio while local market results are measured by the number of class I, class II, and class III banks operating in the market. All structural changes are contrasted with the actual June 1969 banking industry.

In the first result set, the impact of different regulatory policies is analyzed given a fixed assumption of intermediate-sized partner selection. At both statewide and local levels successively less restrictive regulatory policies generate significantly higher levels of concentration. Although all four regulatory policies allow a measured increase in statewide concentration, local market results indicate all policies generate greater competition. In the second experiment, varying partner selection behavior creates mixed outcomes. While preferences for larger partners result in higher statewide concentration, the local markets show little difference among selection behaviors. Again, each market is more competitive when compared to initial structure regardless of behavior. The final result set is created by jointly varying regulatory policies and selection behavior. At the statewide level, the results indicate that regulatory policy and partner size preferences can somewhat offset each other. For example, a very liberal regulatory policy matched with small bank preference yields results very similar to a large bank preference paired with a moderate regulatory policy. On the local level however, little difference is manifest among sets of policies and partner size preferences.

Several interesting conclusions can be derived from the outcomes generated by the New Jersey simulation. First, as with the Yeats study, the results demonstrate that regulatory policy has a measurable impact on banking structure. Second, it is important to differentiate between statewide concentration and local market concentration. A policy that creates a desirable result at one level may have an opposite effect on market structure at a different level. Third, since regulatory policy can be somewhat offset by bank partner selection behavior, allowance for such behavior should be made when policy is formulated.

In summary, the Juncker and Oldfield monte carlo simulation analysis and the Yeats Markov transition process study are each based upon a similar set of general propositions. Both studies assume that stable stochastic processes can adequately model the dynamics of a state's banking market evolution. However, the Juncker and Oldfield analysis attempts to model individual bank expansion behavior while the Yeats study abstracts from microeconomic activity entirely. In addition, each study postulates the existence of discrete bank behavior classes. Such groupings immensely simplify the analysis by focusing on the characteristics of a few general classes of banks rather than examining the particular properties of numerous individual banks in each decision problem.

The two studies have common weaknesses as well as individual strengths. Both models rely upon a heuristic device to generate merger activity. Given the apparent absence of cost motives for multioffice operations, the use of a simple stochastic process to model expansion activity can be defended as a workable expedient that is not contrary to the econometric cost study evidence. In addition, neither analysis incorporates directly a de novo branching mechanism or a device for exploring the impact of various feasible state laws. The Yeats model includes a de novo entry provision that the simulation model does not. Conversely, the Juncker and Oldfield analysis provides for the investigation of both local and statewide changes deriving from regulatory and behavioral alterations that the Yeats study does not. On balance, the simulation methodology appears to be a useful technique for further detailed analysis of banking structure issues.

One shortcoming of the Juncker and Oldfield simulation approach is the arbitrary definitions of regulatory policies and partner selection behavior. In each case, a discrete decision situation for a bank or agency is governed by a simple arbitrary rule. However, such cases lend themselves to a statistical investigation of past decisions by banks and regulators. A combination of discriminant functions like those estimated by Gilbert and the simulation procedure developed by Juncker and Oldfield can give a powerful model for analyzing structural changes in a state's banking industry.

NOTES

1. An excellent summary of early cost studies may be found in Guttentag and Herman [23]. A more recent survey and additional analysis is located in Mullineaux [34]. Particularly complete analyses may be found in Bell and Murphy [3] and Mullineaux [34].

2. Mullineaux [34].

3. Guttentag and Herman [23] pp. 122-124 and Mullineaux [34].

4. All results cited below are from Mullineaux [34].

5. This is true only to the extent that more offices operate under branching regimes than under unit banking laws. Evidence cited by Guttentag and Herman [23] tends to support the hypothesis that liberal branching laws generate more banking facilities *ceterus paribus* than unit banking laws. However, the margin does not appear to be great.

6. Two recent papers by Gilbert [18] and [19] address the same issue.

7. Sinkey [41].

8. Eisenbeis [13].

9. Yeats [45].

10. Juncker and Oldfield [28].

11. For any state, if the percent of total deposits is plotted vertically and the percent of total banks is plotted horizontally, the Gini ratio is defined as the area between a 45-degree line (representing equal shares for all banks) and the Lorenz curve (denoting the actual size distribution of banks) divided by the total area beneath the 45-degree line. Thus the Gini ratio measures the divergence between the actual level of concentration and zero concentration. See Yeats [45] p. 630.

Chapter III

Simulation Methodology

This chapter explains the basic assumptions, construction, and operation of the simulation model that is used to experiment with a variety of banking structure control instruments. In general, the simulation model incorporates several linear or quadratic discriminant equations and regression equations estimated from cross-section, pooled cross-section, or time series data. All regulatory and bank behavior in the model is governed by certain behavioral and environmental assumptions specified below, and by periodic updates of the stored information generated by intermediate simulation results. The simulation equations are based upon data that appear relevant on theoretical and a priori grounds, are available at "reasonable" cost, can be stored and accurately updated in the model, and work well. This eliminates many variables that seem desirable from a theoretical standpoint. However, it is felt that the most relevant factors are included. Moreover, it is not useful for the purposes of this study to estimate equations based upon conditions that cannot be incorporated or duplicated in the simulation. Consequently, most of the estimated equations are less accurate than would be possible in a purely descriptive study. At the same time, the equations are specified and estimated in a manner that allows them to be useful under a wide variety of experimental conditions.

GENERAL ASSUMPTIONS

The major assumptions used in the study are based upon a mixture of economic theory, observation, and information obtained through interviews. While the simulation is considerably simplified through the use of such assumptions, distortions are inevitable. Although some subtle and concealed distortions may persist, rigorous analysis of each assumption coupled with prior experience in constructing such models has probably eliminated the most troublesome possibilities.

Four general assumptions concern the overall construction of the model. The first is directed toward subdividing the bank expansion process into manageable parts. It is hypothesized that bank expansion is governed by three categories of influences: innate bank behavior, regulatory constraints (defined by federal regulatory agencies), and legal options (imposed by state legislators). The regulatory and legal rules are exogenously determined policy instruments that are the subject of the study. These two categories interact with bank behavior through a learning process as banks become aware of an altered environment.

The second assumption relates to banks' internal growth through time. The absence of time series information relating to market composition necessitates a fairly stringent threefold assumption concerning deposit growth rates. First, the only significant changes in the relative total deposit size of individual banks occur through de novo branches or mergers. Second, market growth rates maintain a constant relative ranking vis-à-vis all other markets within the term of the projections. Third, the regulatory agencies' and the banks' perceptions of "bigness" grow at the same rate. Various aspects of this assumption allow estimates based upon 1968 to 1971 deposit sizes and growth rate rankings to be utilized in predicting behavior during the next decade.

The third assumption concerns a difference in decision-making outlook between banks and regulators in the model. Regulatory decisions are based upon absolute magnitudes of decision variables while expansion attempts are based upon relative magnitudes of desirable characteristics. Federal regulators must be concerned with equity and consistency in judging expansion proposals from all over the state. Conversely, banks are faced with choosing a "best" feasible option from a limited set of alternatives. The feasible set may be unique for each bank and quite different for banks in different locations. While there may be some lower absolute limit of desirability in assessing expansion opportunities, this limit is not subject to estimation because of data limitations.

The final assumption concerns the stability of the estimated relationships. The cross-section equations based upon observations in Pennsylvania 1968/1971 are assumed to describe behavior accurately during the course of the simulation.

THE BASIC STRUCTURE OF THE MODEL

The large number and diverse characteristics of commercial banks in Pennsylvania prevent intensive modeling of each organization's independent decision processes. Therefore, individual bank expansion behavior is treated primarily as a stochastic sequence of attempts at de novo branching and merging. However, the use of specific bank and market characteristics coupled with the postulated existence of several broad classes of homogenous behavior allow a considerable measure of regularity to be introduced into overall expansion activity. The intent of the analysis is not to predict that bank A will merge with bank B in some given year. This is unnecessary because similar ultimate market outcomes may result from many different aggregate expansion ensembles. However, given the initial assumptions that drive the model, certain sequences of aggregate expansion activity are more likely than others.

The objective of the simulation is to project distributions of probable competitive structures in local banking markets through randomly generated series of de novo branch and merger proposals. Repeated simulation of the same time period allows distributions of expansion activity under alternative asumptions to be compared despite a lesser degree of accuracy in any particular run. The flow chart presented in Figure 3.1 depicts the model's construction. The top three blocks control simulation replication and the time interval for experimentation. Once these experimental parameters are set, the model generates estimates for the number of acquisitions and de novo branches in the given year and arranges the two types of expansion attempts in a random sequence. Once in this sequence, either a de novo branch or acquisition is indicated. The type of expansion attempt specified determines the path to be followed through the simulation. If an acquisition is indicated, an initiating bank is located. This initiator commences a search for a feasible partner. Feasible partners are defined to be those banks smaller than the initiator that are located in legal geographic expansion regions. Next, each bank in the set of feasible partner banks identified by the initiator is screened through the initiator's perception of operable regulatory policy. Those banks evaluated as likely to meet regulatory approval are termed potential partners and are considered for combinations with the initiator. From this set of potential partners, a particular bank may be chosen if it is deemed attractive enough for acquisition. Finally, a regulatory decision is rendered and all banks adjust their perceptions of regulatory policy following the decision. If at any point the decision processes fail to generate a successful combination of initiator and partner banks, the simulation cycles back to select a new initiator. Once a successful pairing is attained, the relevant bank and market data are updated to reflect the combination. At this point, a new expansion attempt is initiated governed by the random sequence of branches and acquisitions at the beginning of the process.

The de novo branch path operates in a manner similar to the merger procedure. If a de novo branch expansion is specified, the first step is to locate an initiator. This initiator identifies legal expansion regions and evaluates the relevant markets. Based upon a statistical analysis of historical branching activity, a market is selected for the branch. When no market available to the original initiator merits opening a de novo office a new initiator is selected and this bank begins its own market search. This process continues until a de novo branch is established by some initiator. Relevant

SIMULATION FLOW CHART

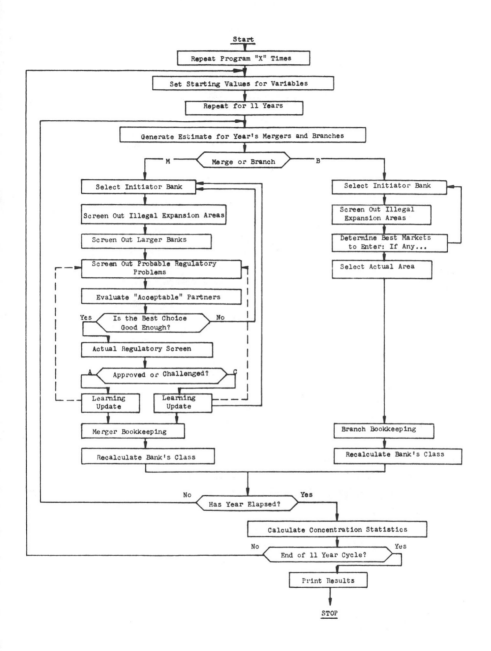

FIGURE 3.1

bank and market data are then revised to reflect the existence of the new office. While no regulatory considerations are built into the de novo branching procedure, provisons for such policy could easily be included in the simulation.

STATISTICAL PROCEDURES

The flow diagram indicates how the simulation consists of parallel paths of sequential choice situations. Within the dual expansion sequences, the choice situations are arranged to replicate the actual merging and de novo branching processes as banks perceive them. Once a course of action is selected, each decision point comprises a set of mutually exclusive alternatives from which, in general, a specific option must be selected. For example, once a merger initiator is specified in the simulation, it must evaluate each merger partner in the set of banks "acceptable" for acquisition. (Note from Figure 3.1 that "acceptable" merger partners are those which are legally feasible, smaller than the initiator, and perceived likely to meet regulatory approval.) Within this set of banks, a discriminant function based upon a statistical analysis of actual past decisions categorizes each potential partner as desirable or undesirable. A particular desirable bank is then chosen.

The choice alternatives comprising each decision situation are assumed to be completely described by a set of relevant variables and the magnitudes of each alternative's characteristics. Therefore, particular decision options (e.g., merger partners) may be presented by their attribute vectors in a multidimensional attributes space. In analyzing historical decisions made in actual choice situations, the variables describing the observed choice alternatives are considered random variables. Depending upon the nature of the decision alternatives' attributes (continuous or discrete, etc.), specific multivariate density functions are assumed to represent the probability distributions from which the observations are drawn. The reconstruction of an actual choice situation also provides ex post information specifying chosen and unchosen alternatives. Hence, each observation can be represented in a coordinate system of attributes and also identified with the chosen or unchosen group.

This decision framework is used for the regulatory decision, initiator specification, merger partner choice, and de novo branch market selection processes.

A reconstruction of the regulatory decision situation might appear as in Figure 3.2. In this simple example, proposed mergers are assumed to be described by two characteristics. Let X_1 represent the deposit size of the initiator bank and X_2 represent the distance in miles between initiator and partner. In this hypothetical sample of observed merger attempts, $\underset{\sim}{A}$ vectors depict mergers actually approved by the regulatory authorities while the $\underset{\sim}{D}$ vectors represent disapproved mergers. The tilde beneath the observations

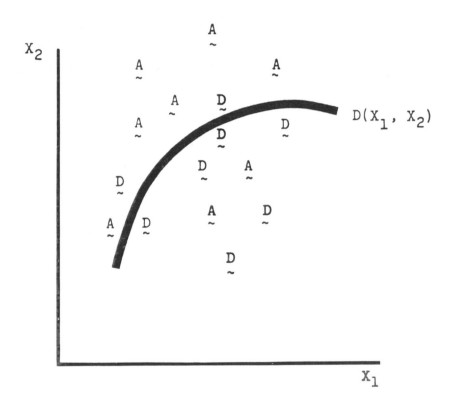

FIGURE 3.2

denotes a vector of characters (X_1, X_2). It is hypothesized that if some function, for example $D(X_1, X_2)$, can be estimated from ex post observations within the sample period that accurately divides the approved and disapproved groups, this function represents the decision rule utilized by federal regulatory agencies in the actual choice situation. Within the simulation, the estimated equation is used to replicate the decision process employed in historical choice situations to specify whether or not a particular hypothetical alternative is chosen.

In estimating a decision equation such as $D(X_1, X_2)$, there may be many functions that more or less accurately divide approved and disapproved alternatives. The criterion used in this analysis to select the "best" function is to choose that which minimizes the probability of misclassifying an observation. The statistical procedure employed for specifying such a decision rule is discriminant analysis. However, there may be no simple linear or quadratic equation (the only functional forms available with discriminant analysis) that divides the groups without any overlap. Briefly, the objective may be denoted as:

$$\text{Min } L = \phi(1/2)\, \pi_2 + \phi(2/1)\, \pi_1$$
$$\{\underset{\sim}{X}\}$$

where

> L: the probability of misclassification;
>
> $\phi\,(g/h)$: the conditional probability of placing an observation in group g when it actually occurs in group h;
>
> π_i: the a priori probability of group membership in group i. That is, π_i is the probability the analyst assigns to an observation's group membership prior to statistical classification.

It can be shown (see Appendix to Chapter V) that the probability of misclassification is minimized if

$$\pi_1 f_1(\underset{\sim}{X}) - \pi_2 f_2(\underset{\sim}{X}) = 0$$

where

> $f_i(\underset{\sim}{X})$: the multivariate attributes density function for group i.

This rule can readily be visualized in a one dimensional characteristics space (Figure 3.3). The area beneath $\pi_i f_i(X)$ is the probability of an observation's membership in group i. The discriminant
rule operates to assign an observation to the group in which it has
the highest probability of occurring.

The point on the X axis denoted by $\pi_1 f_1(X) = \pi_2 f_2(X)$ represents the discriminant rule. In addition, where an observation has
an equal probability of occurring in either group, it is arbitrarily
assigned to group 1. Referring to Figure 3.3, it is evident that an
observation should be classified in group 1 where $\pi_1 f_1(X)$
$> \pi_2 f_2 (X)$ and classified in group 2 where $\pi_1 f_1(X) < \pi_2 f_2(X)$.
Thus, observation A is assigned to group 1 and observation B is
assigned to group 2.

The classification rule may be generalized to the following in a
multidimensional characteristics space, where $\underset{\sim}{X}_j$ represents the
vector of characteristics corresponding to the jth observation. Assign
observation j to group 1

$$\text{if } \underset{\sim}{X}_j: \quad \frac{f_1(\underset{\sim}{X}_j)}{f_2(\underset{\sim}{X}_j)} > \frac{\pi_2}{\pi_1};$$

otherwise assign $\underset{\sim}{X}_j$ to group 2.

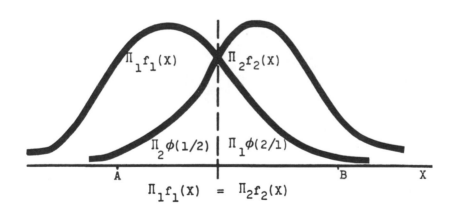

FIGURE 3.3

The four decision processes that govern the basic operations of the simulation all function in a manner analogous to that detailed in the regulatory example above. These choice situations comprise the operations of categorizing banks into classes of expansion initiators, merger partner choice, de novo branch market selection, and merger regulatory decision. If the multivariate classification procedures employed to estimate these decision rules are to function properly, there must exist discrete, mutually exclusive and exhaustive groups in the sets of observations pertaining to each decision situation. To the extent these conditions are violated, classification power diminishes. None of the choice situations reconstructed in the model completely fulfill all the requirements. The specific problems in each are detailed extensively in the section explaining the estimation of the choice procedures. The next two chapters detail the legal and regulatory options that constrain expansion activity.

Chapter IV

Legal Alternatives Employed
in the Model

A state's banking law constrains banks operating in the state to certain legal organizational structures and geographic expansion areas. Although each state's law is unique, the provisions of the different laws are usually grouped into three general categories on the basis of permissable branching activities. Unlimited statewide branching laws place no geographic bounds on mergers and de novo branches. In addition, multibank holding companies are not usually restricted. For example, in California statewide expansion can be accomplished through merging, de novo branching, or holding company acquisitions. However, in Washington statewide merging and de novo branching are legal but multibank holding companies are not. A second expansion law category is generally termed limited branching. States with this type law place geographic limits (for example, only in the initiating bank's home office county) on banks' merging, de novo branching, and holding company activities. The Ohio and Michigan laws contain geographic restrictions on de novo branching and merging but allow statewide multibank holding companies. In other limited branching states like Pennsylvania and Massachusetts, multibank

31

holding companies are illegal. The final legal category is unit banking. In states like Illinois, virtually all forms of multiple office activity are proscribed.

THE PENNSYLVANIA BANKING LAW

Limited branching laws are common in industrialized states. The banking industries in Massachusetts, Michigan, Ohio, and Pennsylvania all operate within the bounds of legally defined constraints on organizational structure and geographic expansion regions. These laws represent legislative compromise between the interests of large, aggressive urban banks and the fears of small, independent rural banks. Thus, small nonmetropolitan banks located beyond the limited expansion areas available from major urban centers are protected from merger or direct de novo branch competition with the large metropolitan banks. The particular branching law in Pennsylvania constrains merger and de novo branch activity to a bank's home office county and adjacent counties. Multiple bank holding companies are illegal.[1]

Pennsylvania provides an especially interesting experimental environment for investigating general banking structure issues. The provisions of the contiguous county branching law (combined with a permissive federal merger regulatory policy) appear to have strongly influenced the existing banking structure.[2] Two effects of these expansion policies are evident. First, Pennsylvania has both a large number of banks and a large yearly number of mergers and de novo branches. Second, most expansion activity occurs in metropolitan areas. In general, the contiguous county law has allowed urban banks to expand rapidly into neighboring suburban areas. While metropolitan areas have become more concentrated, the state law has assured the continuing viability of many small rural banks. Thus, areas displaying the characteristics of a free branching law abut regions that resemble unit banking states. Within this framework of diverse bank behavior, successively more liberal laws are tested in the simulation to gauge the structural impact of a discrete range of legal constraints.

MODES OF EXPANSION IN THE MODEL

Three modes of expansion are possible in the simulation. The assumptions made concerning these alternatives attempt to capture the particular organizational aspects of each type expansion. The specific definitions of mergers, holding company acquisitions, and de novo branches as used in the model are indicated below.

- When two banks merge, the *initiator* is the surviving bank. The acquired bank loses its identity and its offices become branches of the initiator. All future computations concerning the initiator and markets in which it operates are calculated on the basis of the post-merger bank's characteristics.

- A bank absorbed by a holding company loses its ability to merge but maintains its independent de novo branching option. Only the lead bank is also allowed to initiate acquisitions after holding company formation. Regulatory assessment of lead bank acquisitions, both mergers and holding company additions, is based upon overall holding company characteristics. In behavioral calculations, the lead bank considers de novo branch expansions, mergers, and holding company acquisitions on the basis of its own—not holding company—characteristics. However, combined holding company values are used by the lead bank when evaluating the approval likelihood of a proposed acquisition. Banks acquired by the holding company evaluate de novo markets relative to themselves alone.

- When a bank initiates a de novo branch expansion, it is assigned a new branch in the market chosen. This new branch is immediately allocated deposits of $2 million.[3] All future computations concerning the initiating bank or the selected market include the de novo branch information.

In summary, two types of banks are defined. Independent banks and holding company lead banks can branch, merge, or make holding company acquisitions. Holding company member banks (other than the lead bank) can de novo branch only. Holding company acquisitions and mergers are evaluated in an identical fashion by both sets of potential initiators. In addition, the regulatory rule treats them both as mergers.

SPECIFIC LEGAL ALTERNATIVES OF THE MODEL

Different laws allow specific expansion alternatives within strictly defined geographical regions. These legal provisions are rules within the simulation that constrain a bank's choice set when considering merger partners, de novo branch markets, or holding company acquisitions. Those expansion alternatives disallowed by a state law do not enter into a bank's set of feasible choices.

Four separate state laws are defined for use in the model. These are: statewide de novo branching and merging, statewide holding companies with contiguous county branching and merging, district merging and de novo branching, and the present contiguous county law. These options represent state laws similar to those enacted recently in other states or frequently mentioned as likely alternatives for Pennsylvania.

The·simulation's statewide law is similar to laws existing in Washington and Louisiana. Banks are allowed to merge and branch anywhere within the state but multibank holding companies are illegal. An alternative statewide expansion law tested in the model contains provisions similar to the Ohio and Michigan banking laws. The particular form investigated in the simulation is designed to maintain certain features of the existing Pennsylvania law. Thus, statewide expansion through multibank holding companies is allowed but mergers and de novo branches are limited to a bank's home office and contiguous counties. It is assumed that banks merge where such activity is legal and make holding company acquisitions elsewhere. Therefore, while the statewide branching law defined in the model proscribes multibank holding companies, it is not materially different from the unlimited branching laws in California and Connecticut. In these states, few multibank holding company acquisitions occur since mergers are permissable.[4]

For the purposes of simulating a district expansion alternative, two hypothetical state banking districts are constructed for use with the district branching law. The state is roughly bisected with the district line almost entirely following county lines. In addition, the district border follows rivers, national forests, and other natural boundaries in many areas. District 1 comprises Philadelphia and Harrisburg, and district 2 contains the western portion of the state including Altoona and Pittsburgh. A bank may merge or branch de novo anywhere within its home office district but multibank holding companies are illegal. It is also assumed that a "grandfather" clause allows the maintenance of any preestablished expansion region beyond an initiating bank's home office district. That is, banks may expand into any county that was allowable under the contiguous county law. Thus, the districts overlap to some limited extent. The purpose of testing this law is to examine the impact of wide area limited expansion where banks in the major metropolitan areas cannot directly compete. The final law investigated in the model is the present contiguous county branching law with no multibank holding companies. Forecasts made with this law provide a control prediction to gauge the impact on banking structure of the other less restrictive laws.

Thus, the framework for experimentation is the existing banking structure in Pennsylvania. Given this structure, four successively less restrictive laws ranging from the present contiguous county law to an unlimited statewide branching law are defined for experimentation. Expansion activity is simulated under each law in conjunction with alternative regulatory policies to measure both the joint and independent influences of legal and regulatory constraints. The alternative regulatory policies tested concurrently with the four laws are detailed in the next chapter.

NOTES

1. Other industrialized states with limited branching laws have had a similar experience, although expansion activity has not generally been as vigorous as in Pennsylvania. New York, Massachusetts, Michigan, New Jersey, Ohio and Pennsylvania together accounted for between one-half and one-third of total yearly

bank combinations between 1969 and 1976. Data supplied by the Board of Governors of the Federal Reserve System.

2. A bank holding company is a corporation that owns one or more commercial banks. In a one-bank holding company, only one-bank is owned.

3. This is based upon a survey of average de novo branch performance after two years. Also, discussions with bankers indicated that, in most cases, this is the minimum desirable branch size. Full size is assigned instantaneously to avoid growth routines. Branches are assumed to grow at the market rate after the initial deposit allocation.

4. In California, there were six multibank holding company acquisitions between 1960 and 1972, but there were 99 mergers. In Connecticut, there has been virtually no multibank holding company activity (three banks formed a holding company in 1970) but 32 mergers. Data supplied by the Board of Governors of the Federal Reserve System.

Chapter V

Regulatory Policy

Federal regulation of bank mergers and holding company acquisitions is a potentially useful instrument for influencing banking market structure. Virtually every proposed combination between banks must obtain prior regulatory approval from appropriate federal agencies. This chapter describes how the regulatory policy governing such combinations is specified for experimentation in the simulation model. Three mutually exclusive policies are defined. Each is designed to represent a reasonable policy that the regulatory agencies might feasibly implement. One policy reflects the present rules for bank combinations. Two alternative policies represent hypothetical shifts in regulatory focus. The overall objective is to define rules that illuminate the joint impact of regulatory policy and state banking law on banking structure evolution.

INSTITUTIONAL ASPECTS OF FEDERAL REGULATIONS

Regulation of bank combinations involves several independent federal agencies. The Bank Merger Act of 1960 specifies that no bank insured by the Federal Deposit Insurance Corporation

(FDIC) can merge or consolidate through acquisition with any other bank without prior written approval of the appropriate federal authorities. Briefly, this means approval must be obtained from: 1) the Comptroller of the Currency if the resultant bank is a national bank; 2) the Board of Governors of the Federal Reserve System if the resultant organization is a state chartered member bank; and 3) the FDIC if the resultant bank is a nonmember insured bank.[1] In addition, under the Bank Holding Company Act of 1956, all proposed acquisitions of banks by bank holding companies must have prior written approval from the Board of Governors of the Federal Reserve System. Holding company acquisitions and mergers are treated identically by the Board when the competitive impact of a proposed combination is evaluated. That is, the multibank organization is treated as one large bank. Finally, the United States Department of Justice may challenge in court any merger or acquisition previously approved by a regulatory agency.[2] In the discussion below, the term "regulatory agencies" refers to all three federal agencies and the Justice Department.

Regulatory decisions concerning mergers and holding company acquisitions focus on a proposed combination's impact on competition in local banking markets. The emphasis on local markets derives from the regulatory agencies' common desire to monitor closely any proposed expansion's likely effect on the small business and household customers of commercial banks. These categories comprise the bulk of bank customers and also include the least mobile users of unique commercial bank services.[3] It is assumed that large demand depositors and commercial borrowers are able to search extensive geographic regions to find adequate banking accommodation. Conversely, small commercial borrowers and small household and commercial demand depositors are viewed as confined to local banking alternatives. The resultant regulatory strategy aims to encourage competition in local markets (within certain limits dictated by safety considerations). If local markets are highly competitive, it follows that a plenitude of banking options is also available to large customers. In addition, insuring competitive production of unique commercial bank services also implies competition in the provision of other nonunique services.

This includes time deposits, mortgages, and personal loans. Regulatory policy concentrated on the most narrow market category generates competition at all levels.

On the one hand, the existence of discrete and mutually exclusive local banking markets is extremely unlikely. Instead, each bank's customers are drawn from areas that overlap other banks' drawing regions. Competition occurs in a continuum across a wide area with each bank's rivalrous influence on other banks diminishing with distance. On the other hand, banks can generally be grouped into approximate market areas where the dominant local influence emanates from a central cluster of banks. Judgment must be used to place banks located in border regions in one neighboring market or another. By analyzing several variables—including deposit rates, loan rates, and banking hours—a Federal Reserve Bank of Philadelphia study identifies 55 local banking markets in Pennsylvania.[4] These markets are regional areas encompassing townships and trade areas grouped on commercial and demographic bases rather than county lines. The use of natural barriers and low population areas to separate markets wherever possible somewhat mitigates the arbitrary nature of discrete market boundaries. Figure 5.1, a map delineating Pennsylvania's local banking markets, appears on the next page.

Once mutually exclusive local markets are defined, objective characteristics of market structure can be enumerated. These characteristics attempt to summarize a market's competitive arrangements and detail individual bank's contributions to overall market performance. Variables such as a bank's local market rank, size, and proximity to other banks are extensively used in regulatory decisions. A statistical analysis employing these and related measures forms the core of the following sections.

AN ANALYSIS OF RECENT
REGULATORY DECISIONS

The historical analysis is limited to formal merger proposals by banks in Third District Pennsylvania between 1966 and 1971. Fifty-two merger attempts were chosen for study. This included 11

LOCAL PENNSYLVANIA BANKING MARKETS

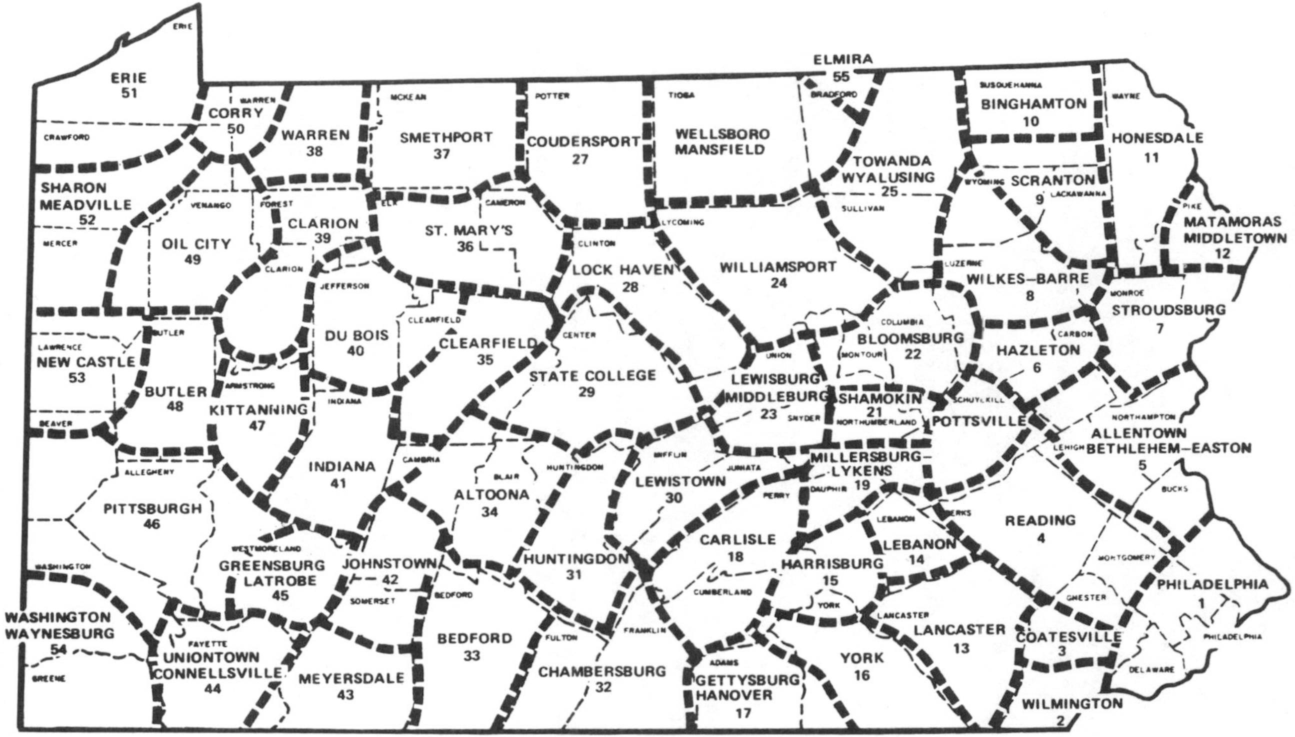

SOURCE: Cynthia A. Glassman (18).

MAP 5.1

mergers that were denied or challenged in court (virtually all since 1966) and 41 bank mergers that comprised all approved and unchallenged mergers identified from 1968 to 1971. It is difficult to ascertain whether this is a representative sample of attempted mergers during this period. Few controversial merger applications reach the stage where regulatory agencies formally reject them. In many cases, tentative combinations proposed in informal queries are discouraged by the relevant authorities even before formal proceedings. Such cases are exceptionally difficult to identify and analyze. Consequently, the proportions of acceptances and formally blocked mergers do not reflect the a priori probabilities that any observed merger proposal will be in some manner deterred. The a priori probabilities employed were obtained through discussions with regulatory authorities at the Federal Bank of Philadelphia. The probability of disapproval is specified as $\pi_R = 1/3$, the probability of approval is $\pi_A = 2/3$.[5]

The basic assumptions underlying the historical analysis concern the stability of the decision rule during the time period examined and consistency among the regulatory agencies. It is impossible to assess whether the historical rule remained constant during the time period investigated. However, in examining the individual merger cases, nothing that could be deemed a substantial shift in priorities of precedent was ascertained. Moreover, experience over several years of participating in the regulatory process supports this assertion. The sample of denials and challenges was too small to establish this statistically.

Consistency among the regulatory agencies is somewhat easier to gauge. There is extensive communication and discussion among the agencies concerning each merger. In most cases, all agencies prepare standardized analyses of the proposed combination utilizing agreed-upon terminology. In addition, the Comptroller, FDIC, and Federal Reserve Board generally have not challenged proposed combinations directly. Most frequently, an applicant for a merger deemed "substantially adverse" to competition is advised that U.S. Department of Justice intervention is very probable. Among the 11 blocked mergers studied, nine were approved by the responsible regulatory agency and subsequently challenged successfully by the Justice Department. Hence, it is essentially the Justice Department's decision rule that is investigated.

For each historical merger proposal studied, the analyses prepared at the time by the Federal Reserve Bank of Philadelphia and the Department of Justice were examined. In all cases these analyses were noticeably consistent. In each case, the proposed merger was described in terms of a large number of proxy variables attempting to summarize the competitive effects of the merger. Seven characteristics of each proposed combination that were commonly incorporated in the evaluation of each merger are extracted. Either identical or directly comparable variables are employed in this study. These can be generally categorized into two groups, size variables and proximity variables.

Where inconsistencies between merger analyses prepared by the separate agencies occurred, they were minor in all cases. For example, the definition of the relevant geographical markets of the banks frequently varied somewhat. In all cases, the Pennsylvania market classification scheme recently developed by the Federal Reserve Bank of Philadelphia is used. This approximates the market definitions employed at the time by the regulatory agencies, especially the FDIC and Department of Justice.

The principle governing the choice of variables for analyzing regulatory decisions is to include those that are apparently important, measurable, and can be maintained in the simulation. A listing of the characteristics utilized is included below.

Proximity Variables
X_1: Distance between home office of applicant and other bank.
X_2: Number of offices of both banks in same markets
÷ Number of offices of both banks total.

(Numerator excludes home market offices unless both home offices are in the same market.)

Size Variables
X_3: Rank of applicant bank in its primary market
X_4: Rank of other bank in its home office market
X_5: Number of offices of applicant bank
X_6: Number of offices of other bank

X_7: Deposits of other bank in its home office market
÷ Total deposits in other bank's home office market.

No concentration ratio measure is included, for two reasons. First, no consistent concentration ratio is utilized in the actual merger analyses. In some markets only three or four competitors operate; in others, 40 or 50 separate banking organizations conduct business. No simple two-, four-, or eight-firm concentration ratio is widely applicable. Second, operational considerations render the use of such measures extremely difficult. Many merging banks operate primarily in the same market. Defining a separate concentration ratio for each bank merely repeats the same number twice. This introduces excessive collinearity among the variables. An identical problem also occurs with several other characteristics. To avoid such collinearity problems, alternate variables are included. For example, in the sample utilized, total deposit variables are almost perfectly collinear with X_5 and X_6, the number of offices variables. However, use of X_5 and X_6 leads to better separation between the groups. This is probably because the number of offices variables measure a bank's propensity to expand as well as its size. Chapter III briefly detailed how a discriminant rule could be expressed as an inequality between two ratios:

assign observation j to group reject if $\dfrac{fR(\underset{\sim}{X}_j)}{fA(\underset{\sim}{X}_j)} < \dfrac{\pi_A}{\pi_R}$;

otherwise assign j to group accept;

where $\underset{\sim}{X}_j$: the vector of the jth merger attempt's characteristics,

$$\underset{\sim}{X}'_j = (X_{1j},\ X_{2j},\ X_{3j},\ X_{4j},\ X_{5j},\ X_{6j},\ X_{7j});$$

fg($\underset{\sim}{X}$): the multivariate density function of group g;

   π_g: the a priori probability of an observation's membership in group g. π_A is the prior probability that a merger is acceptable, π_R is the prior probability that it will be rejected.

Taking the natural logarithm of each side of the inequality yields

(1) $\ln[fR(\underset{\sim}{X}_j)] - \ln[fA(\underset{\sim}{X}_j)] < \ln\dfrac{\pi_A}{\pi_R}.$

Each group's distribution of merger characteristics is assumed to be multivariate normal. This allows specification of a precise functional form for the discriminant rule. (See this chapter's appendix for a more rigorous derivation of this material.) After rearranging terms, the inequality can be written as

$$(2) \quad \underset{\sim}{X}'_j \left(\sum{}_R^{-1} - \sum{}_A^{-1} \right) \underset{\sim}{X}_j - 2 \left(\underset{\sim}{\mu}'_R \sum{}_R^{-1} - \underset{\sim}{\mu} \sum{}_A^{-1} \right) \underset{\sim}{X}_j$$
$$+ \left(\underset{\sim}{\mu}' \sum{}_R^{-1} \underset{\sim}{\mu}_R - \underset{\sim}{\mu}'_A \sum{}_A^{-1} \underset{\sim}{\mu}_A \right) - \ln \left| \sum{}_A \cdot \sum{}_R^{-1} \right| > -2\ln \frac{\pi_A}{\pi_R}.$$

where $\sum_g$: the covariance matrix of group g;
$\underset{\sim}{\mu}_g$: the vector of means for group g.

To simplify the expression of the estimated discriminant rule, inequality (2) can be written in a simple quadratic form:
assign $\underset{\sim}{X}_j$ to group reject if

$$\underset{\sim}{X}'_j D \underset{\sim}{X}_j - 2\underset{\sim}{b}'_j \underset{\sim}{X}_j + c_1 - c_2 > -2\ln\left(\frac{\pi_A}{\pi_R}\right) ;$$

otherwise assign X_j to group accept.

The estimated values for the historical decision rule appear below.

$$\underset{\sim}{b} = \begin{vmatrix} 7.4142 \\ 1.4722 \\ 0.67522 \\ 0.55734 \\ -0.42100 \\ -0.13391 \\ 0.34871 \end{vmatrix}$$

$$D^{-1} = \begin{vmatrix} -2.1150 & 0.0 & 0.0 & 0.0 & 0.0 & 0.0 & 0.0 \\ -0.6052 & -0.1045 & 0.0 & 0.0 & 0.0 & 0.0 & 0.0 \\ 0.6445 & -0.0870 & -0.8120 & 0.0 & 0.0 & 0.0 & 0.0 \\ -0.4252 & 0.1172 & 0.1217 & -0.1595 & 0.0 & 0.0 & 0.0 \\ 0.2333 & 0.0017 & 0.0185 & 0.0785 & 0.0120 & 0.0 & 0.0 \\ -0.4674 & 0.0609 & 0.3814 & -0.1587 & 0.0346 & 0.0264 & 0.0 \\ -0.1009 & -0.0178 & -0.0512 & -0.0120 & 0.0047 & 0.0097 & -0.003 \end{vmatrix}$$

$c_1 = 2.527$
$c_2 = -8.5411$
$\ln \frac{\pi_A}{\pi_R} = 0.69315$

Variable	Percent Discriminating Power
X_1	19.56
X_2	4.85
X_3	10.78
X_4	15.36
X_5	26.60
X_6	16.79
X_7	6.07

An F test of the null hypothesis of group covariance matrix equality yields F = 2.606 with 28 and 1,181.3 degrees of freedom.[6] This allows rejection of the null hypothesis at a .01 significance level. Similarly, an F test of group mean vector equality gives F = 4.448 with 7 and 44 degrees of freedom. The null hypothesis of mean vector equality can be rejected at a .01 significance level. Both results support the discriminating power of the rule used.

Using the estimated equation to classify the historical sample generates the table below. Entries on the array's main diagonal represent correct classifications and off-diagonal elements denote misclassified observations.

	Predicted Reject	Predicted Accept
Actual Reject	10	1
Actual Accept	3	38

For example, 11 merger proposals were actually rejected by the regulatory authorities. In testing the equation, 10 of these merger attempts are classified reject [row 1, column 1 or cell (1, 1)] and 1 is classified accept (1, 2). Thus the (1, 2) entry denotes a merger proposal incorrectly classified by the estimated equation. Similarly, 41 merger proposals were actually rejected by the regulatory agencies. In this group, the estimated equation misclassified 3 proposals as acceptances (2, 1) and correctly classified 38 observations (2, 2). The estimated rule clearly works quite well as a statistical representation of recent regulatory procedures. Unfortunately, the sample is too small for experiments with a hold-out group.

TWO HYPOTHETICAL REGULATORY POLICIES

To estimate the two hypothetical regulatory policies, a series of 90 representative merger proposals was constructed. These cases included values for each of the seven characteristics found significant and useful in the historical study. In addition, other items of information were provided. Three economists at the Federal Reserve Bank of Philadelphia independently rendered accept or reject opinions on each hypothetical merger according to criteria defined for the different regulatory policies.

The two hypothetical rules are designed to represent nonextreme extensions of historical policy. For the *actual competition* rule, the ground rules specify that a policy should be formulated that promotes greater direct competition among banks. Protection of individual banks is less important than fostering the growth of viable competitors. Thus mergers between small and medium-sized banks operating in the same market would not necessarily be denied if several banking alternatives remained in the market. The *potential competition* rule is focused toward a policy that the federal regulatory agencies, particularly the FDIC and Department of Justice, are trying to establish as enforceable. Under this rule, the objective is to prevent an acquisition either where there is substantial direct competition between the banks (like the historical policy) or where future competition is likely. Hence, if it is considered probable that one bank in a proposed combination can or will enter the other's market through de novo branching, the combination is prevented even though the organizations do not directly compete at the time of the proposal.

The majority opinion in each merger case was taken as the regulatory ruling on the individual hypothetical combinations. This yielded two sets of decisions. The actual competition set contained 58 approvals and 32 denials. The potential competition set comprised 40 approvals and 50 denials. Each set was independently used to estimate a classification rule corresponding to the decision criteria specified for the hypothetical regulatory policies.

Linear and quadratic procedures were both tested. In both cases, quadratic methods produced superior classification. Additional variables, including deposit size and number of competitors in the second bank's market, were tested with little increase in discriminating power. Only the seven original variables are maintained in the analysis. The actual competition results are given first. Both equations are presented in the format specified for the historical classification rule.

Actual Competition Classification Rule

$$\underset{\sim}{b} = \begin{vmatrix} 0.3097 \\ 0.6564 \\ 0.8382 \\ 1.7526 \\ 0.0559 \\ 0.0019 \\ 0.3546 \end{vmatrix}$$

$$D^{-1} = \begin{vmatrix} -0.0113 & 0.0 & 0.0 & 0.0 & 0.0 & 0.0 & 0.0 \\ -0.0453 & -0.0607 & 0.0 & 0.0 & 0.0 & 0.0 & 0.0 \\ -0.0296 & -0.1410 & -0.0989 & 0.0 & 0.0 & 0.0 & 0.0 \\ 0.0510 & 0.2660 & 0.0638 & -0.3353 & 0.0 & 0.0 & 0.0 \\ -0.0030 & -0.0125 & 0.0054 & 0.0063 & 0.0006 & 0.0 & 0.0 \\ -0.0078 & 0.0012 & 0.0044 & 0.0047 & -0.0029 & 0.0147 & 0.0 \\ 0.0073 & 0.0462 & 0.0181 & -0.1052 & 0.0021 & -0.0046 & -0.0095 \end{vmatrix}$$

$c_1 = 1.3596$

$c_2 = 10.689$

$\ln \dfrac{\pi_A}{\pi_R} = 0.69315$

Variable	Percent Discriminating Power
X_1	5.30
X_2	39.60
X_3	13.73
X_4	14.04
X_5	8.10
X_6	10.44
X_7	8.72

The null hypothesis can be rejected at a .01 level of significance. An F test of group mean vector equality gives $F = 10.9835$ with 7 and 82 degrees of freedom. This allows rejection of the null hypothesis of mean vector equality at a .01 level of significance. The table below indicates the classification results of using the discriminant function to group the members of the sample.

	Predicted Reject	Predicted Accept
Actual Reject	27	5
Actual Accept	6	52

As before, entries on the main diagonal represent correctly classified observations.

Potential Competition Classification Rule

$$\underset{\sim}{b} = \begin{vmatrix} 0.2835 \\ 0.6666 \\ 0.8772 \\ 0.8681 \\ -0.0590 \\ -0.1870 \\ -0.0028 \end{vmatrix}$$

$$D^{-1} = \begin{vmatrix} -0.0074 & 0.0 & 0.0 & 0.0 & 0.0 & 0.0 & 0.0 \\ -0.0310 & -0.0371 & 0.0 & 0.0 & 0.0 & 0.0 & 0.0 \\ -0.0039 & -0.0244 & -0.1017 & 0.0 & 0.0 & 0.0 & 0.0 \\ 0.0039 & 0.0119 & -0.0672 & -0.0803 & 0.0 & 0.0 & 0.0 \\ -0.0121 & 0.0009 & 0.0150 & -0.0221 & 0.0206 & 0.0 & 0.0 \\ -0.0238 & -0.0057 & -0.0195 & 0.0213 & 0.0276 & 0.0880 & 0.0 \\ -0.0018 & -0.0052 & 0.0019 & 0.0015 & -0.0006 & 0.0017 & 0.0003 \end{vmatrix}$$

$c_1 = 0.0395$

$c_2 = 4.5925$

$\ln \dfrac{\pi_A}{\pi_R} = 0.69315$

An F test of the null hypothesis of group covariance matrix equality yields $F = 5.588$ with 28 and 14,677.2 degrees of freedom.

Variable	Percent Discriminating Power
X_1	22.48
X_2	2.56
X_3	12.36
X_4	21.30
X_5	20.79
X_6	13.44
X_7	7.07

The F test of the null hypothesis of group covariance matrix equality yields F = 13.2286 with 28 and 24,337.4 degrees of freedom. This allows rejection of the null hypothesis at a .01 significance level. Similarly, an F test of group mean vector equality yields an F = 5.9295 that allows rejection of the null hypothesis of equality at a .01 significance level.

Classification results for the potential competition rule are indicated in the table below.

	Predicted Reject	Predicted Accept
Actual Reject	38	12
Actual Accept	8	32

The equations do not operate perfectly, especially the two hypothetical policy rules. For the historical rule, misclassification reflects inconsistencies in decision making and the special characteristics of each merger that are not captured by the variables employed. The use of majority decisions for the hypothetical policies is an effort to mitigate individual biases and inconsistencies, but this is not an error-free procedure. This is especially so because only three opinions were sought and no greater weight is attached to unanimous decisions.

It is interesting that interactions between various size and proximity variables enhance classifying power in all three decision rules. This would be expected if there is a size-distance trade off in bank merger regulation. That is, combinations of larger institutions do not adversely affect competition, actual or potential, if the organizations operate at a sufficient distance from one another. This reflects the presumed local nature of much bank competition, especially among small and moderate-sized organizations.

POLICY CHANGES IN THE SIMULATION MODEL

Changes in regulatory policy are incorporated in the simulation by specifying a different operable policy equation. Banks are assumed to learn of a regulatory change as merger proposals are submitted and decisions rendered. Adjustments in the banks' regulatory screen are accomplished through a discrete learning routine represented by a simple difference equation. This learning routine operates on the banks' perceived merger screen by altering the equation's coefficients. Let:

$$(3) \qquad P_R = \underset{\sim}{X}' D_R^{-1} \underset{\sim}{X} + b_R' \underset{\sim}{X} + c_{1R} + c_{2R}$$

represent the operable regulatory policy;

$$(4) \qquad S_j = \underset{\sim}{X}' D_B^{-1} \underset{\sim}{X} + b_B' \underset{\sim}{X} + c_{1B} + c_{2B}$$

represents the banks' perceived merger partner screen. The learning equation operates as a difference equation with learning rate (a), where $0 \leqslant a \leqslant 1$.

$$(5) \qquad S_j = (So - P_R)(a)^j + P_R$$

and S_o: the banks' initial merger screen;

$\quad\quad\,\,\, S_j$: the merger partner screen following the jth merger attempt after a policy change;

$\quad\quad\, P_R$: the operable regulatory screen.

All banks share an identical merger partner screen and learning rate. It is assumed that the learning rate (a) is partially a regulatory policy variable. When a = 0 instantaneous learning occurs; when a = 1 no learning is manifest. Presumably, regulatory agencies can determine to some extent how fast banks learn through information dissemination. In the simulation, various learning rates were tested. The results presented in Chapters VII and VIII use a value of a = 0.90.

AN EXAMPLE OF REGULATORY DECISION MAKING

The way in which the regulatory decision procedures operate in the simulation is depicted in the diagrams below. Figure 5.2A reproduces the regulatory decision portion of the merger expansion path in the simulation flow diagram (Chapter III, Figure 3.1). Figures 5.2B and 5.2C represent the same decision situation in a simplified two dimensional characteristics space of the choice alternatives. Two possible regulatory rules are displayed.

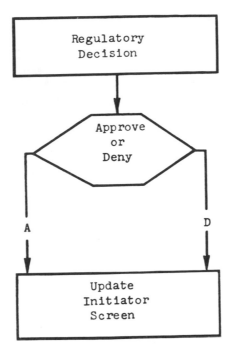

FIGURE 5.2A

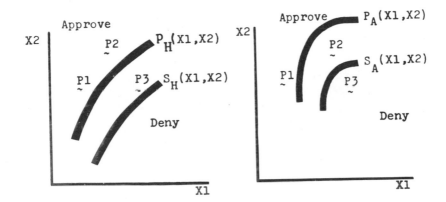

FIGURE 5.2B   **FIGURE 5.2C**

The simulation decision process proceeds by generating a hypothetical combination of initiator and partner banks and testing the proposed merger against the operative regulatory policy. In Figure 5.2B, $P_H(X_1, X_2)$ depicts the regulatory decision rule estimated from historical data. The function $S_H(X_1, X_2)$ represents the merger partner screen equation used by initiating banks while the historical policy is operative. Note that $P_H(X_1, X_2)$ and $S_H(X_1, X_2)$ have the same slope but differ by a constant value. This is due to the different a priori approval probabilities perceived by initiators and regulators. An alternative regulatory policy $P_A(X_1, X_2)$ estimated from questionnaire information is displayed. The function $S_A(X_1, X_2)$ depicts the initators' regulatory screen equation that eventually becomes operative with $P_A(X_1, X_2)$. Thus the initiators' screen gradually (or rapidly, depending on the value of the adjustment rate (a) in the learning procedure) moves from $S_H(X_1, X_2)$ to $S_A(X_1, X_2)$ when regulatory policy shifts from $P_H(X_1, X_2)$ to $P_A(X_1, X_2)$.

In Figure 5.2B, three proposed mergers generated within the simulation are depicted. (Actually only one merger proposal at a time is considered in the regulatory decision portion of the model.) On the basis of the statistical analysis of regulatory decisions, the estimated function $P_H(X_1, X_2)$ approves proposals P_1 and P_2 and disapproves proposal P_3. Figure 5.2C represents the hypothetical rule's operation. If this rule is operable, proposal P_1 is approved and proposals P_2 and P_3 are disapproved. Thus different regulatory policies may render contrary decisions on merger proposals. In this fashion alternative regulatory policies may measurably influence ultimate banking structure.

In summary, three regulatory policies are defined for experimentation in the simulation. Like the state laws previously defined, each regulatory policy is designed to represent an actual or feasible alternative that captures the complex nature of policy decisions. Each policy is independently tested with each of the four state laws discussed in Chapter IV. This creates twelve regulatory-legal environments to explicate the joint and separate impacts of the various structural control instruments. To complete the model's specification for testing such instruments, the nature of bank expansion behavior must be detailed. This is the subject of the next chapter.

NOTES

1. Kreps and Pugh [30] p. 251–252.
2. Fusilier and Darnell [16] p. 145–146.
3. Guttentag and Herman [23] p. 10.
4. Glassman [20].
5. The discriminant analysis procedure used in this study requires a prior probability of group membership.
6. Noninteger degrees of freedom occur because degrees of freedom are indirectly computed with an approximation formula. See Eisenbeis and Avery [12].

APPENDIX

Classification with Multivariate Normal Variables*

The criterion employed to obtain a "good" classification procedure is to minimize the expected probability of misclassification. Formally, the problem can be stated as follows.
Given:

Two populations: P_1 P_2,
Vector of characteristics: $\underset{\sim}{X}' = (X_1, X_2 \ldots X_n)$,
Density functions: $f_1(\underset{\sim}{X})$ and $f_2(\underset{\sim}{X})$,
A priori probabilities: $\pi_1, \pi_2 ; \pi_1 + \pi_2 = 1$,
Decision rule: $\underset{\sim}{X}$ space divided into two regions R_1 and R_2 :
  if $\underset{\sim}{X}_j$ falls in R_1, the observation is classified in P_1
  if $\underset{\sim}{X}_j$ falls in R_2, the observation is classified in P_2.

To minimize the expected probability of misclassification, the objective function is specified as

1)
$$\underset{\{\underset{\sim}{X}\}}{\text{Min M}} = \phi(1/2)\pi_2 + \phi(2/1)\pi_1$$

where $\phi(g/h)$ is the probability of assigning an observation to group g, given that it arose from group h
and

2) $\quad \phi(1/2) = \int_{R_1} f_2 (\underset{\sim}{X}) \, d\underset{\sim}{X}$

3) $\quad \phi(2/1) = \int_{R_2} f_1 (\underset{\sim}{X}) \, d\underset{\sim}{X}.$

The problem may be restated as

4) $\quad \underset{\{\underset{\sim}{X}\}}{\text{Min}} M = \pi_2 \int_{R_1} f_2 (\underset{\sim}{X}) \, d\underset{\sim}{X} + \pi_1 \int_{R_2} f_1 (\underset{\sim}{X}) \, d\underset{\sim}{X}.$

Rearranging terms, one obtains

5) $\quad M = \int_{R_1} [\pi_1 f_1 (\underset{\sim}{X}) - \pi_2 f_2 (\underset{\sim}{X})] \, d\underset{\sim}{X}$
$\quad\quad\quad + \pi_2 \int f_2 (\underset{\sim}{X}) \, d\underset{\sim}{X}$

where

6) $\quad \int_{R_1} f_2 (\underset{\sim}{X}) d\underset{\sim}{X} = 1 - \int_R f_2 (\underset{\sim}{X}) d\underset{\sim}{X}$
$\quad\quad\quad = \int f_2 (\underset{\sim}{X}) d\underset{\sim}{X} - \int_{R_2} f_2 (\underset{\sim}{X}) d\underset{\sim}{X}.$

Since the last term on the right hand side of equation (5) is a positive constant, the expression as a whole is minimized if R_2 is defined as the set of $\underset{\sim}{X}$s for which

7) $\quad [\pi_1 f_1 (\underset{\sim}{X}) - \pi_2 f_2 (\underset{\sim}{X})] \leqslant 0.$

Simplifying expression (7), one obtains the classification rule:

$$\text{assign to } P_1 \text{ if } R_1 : \frac{f_1 (\underset{\sim}{X})}{f_2 (\underset{\sim}{X})} \leqslant \frac{\pi_2}{\pi_1} ;$$

$$\text{assign to } P_2 \text{ if } R_2 : \frac{f_1 (\underset{\sim}{X})}{f_2 (\underset{\sim}{X})} < \frac{\pi_2}{\pi_1} .$$

---

* The theoretical development presented in this section follows closely and is completely derived from J. Johnston, [27] pp. 334–336 and Robert A. Eisenbeis and Paul R. Avery [12].

The precise classification rules can be obtained by assuming $f_1(X)$ and $f_2(X)$ are multivariate normal densities with mean vectors μ_1 and μ_2 and covariance matrices Σ_1 and Σ_2. Take the natural logarithm of density ratios in the classification rule to obtain

8) $\quad \ln \dfrac{f_1(X)}{f_2(X)} = \ln \dfrac{\dfrac{1}{K^{1/2}|\Sigma_1|^{1/2}} \exp - 1/2[(X - \mu_1)'\Sigma_1^{-1}(X - \mu_1)]}{\dfrac{1}{K^{1/2}|\Sigma_1|^{1/2}} \exp - 1/2[(X - \mu_1)'\Sigma_2^{-1}(X - \mu_2)]}$

and

9) $\quad \ln \dfrac{f_1(X)}{f_2(X)} = 1/2\ln |\Sigma_2 \cdot \Sigma_1^{-1}| - 1/2[(X - \mu_1)' \Sigma_1^{-1}(X - \mu_1)$
$\quad\quad\quad\quad - (X - \mu_2)' \Sigma_2^{-1}(X - \mu_2)].$

Multiplying equation (9) by (-2), the decision rule for group 1 may be expressed as the inequality
assign to P_1 if R_1 :

10) $\quad X'(\Sigma_1^{-1} - \Sigma_2^{-1})X| - 2(\mu'\Sigma_1^{-1} - \mu_2\Sigma_2^{-1})X$
$\quad\quad + [\mu'_1 \Sigma_1^{-1}\mu_1 - \mu_2 \Sigma_2^{-1}\mu_2] - \ln |\Sigma_2 \cdot \Sigma_2^{-1}| \leqslant \ln \dfrac{\pi_2}{\pi_1} \, ;$

assign to P_2 if R_2 : the strict inequality above is reversed.
   If $\Sigma_1 = \Sigma_2$, the first term on the left hand side of the decision rule becomes zero. Also where $\Sigma_1 = \Sigma_2$,

$\quad \ln |\Sigma_2 \cdot \Sigma_1^{-1}| = \ln |I| = 0.$

That is, if the multivariate density functions possess equal covariance matrices, the decision rule reduces to a linear expression (minus one constant). Conversely, if $\Sigma_1 \neq \Sigma_2$, a quadratic decision rule is necessary. Thus, in determining the form of discrimant function to be employed, a test of the covariance matrices is critical.

Chapter VI

The Behavior of Merging
and Branching Banks

The evolution of a state's industry is jointly influenced by the interaction of opposing forces in the simulation. The exogeneously determined legislative and regulatory instruments discussed in Chapters IV and V are designed to constrain or channel evolution into outcomes preferred by structural control agencies.[1] In opposition, the active force that causes change in the banking industry derives from the desired external expansion behavior of individual banks. The innate behavior that banks display in selecting combination partners and markets for new offices is this chapter's subject. The objective is to estimate behavioral equations for the simulation that are general enough to operate accurately under the various policy-legal alternatives previously defined. To this end, several data screening and transformation techniques are undertaken to delete the effects of existing law and policy on banks' observed expansion activity. Four aspects of bank-generated evolution are modeled. These are initiating bank classification, acquisition candidate selection, de novo branch market choice, and elapsed time accounting.

The analysis of merger regulation in the preceding chapter illustrates that decision rules can be specified successfully by

defining choice alternatives with vectors of descriptive characteristics. A similar approach is used in this chapter. In the investigation of expansion initiation, acquisition partner selection, and de
novo branch market choice, various bank and market characteristics are employed to estimate expansion behavior equations. Since
many of the variables used in these equations are not normally
distributed, modified estimation procedures must be employed.
This chapter's appendix gives a detailed explanation of the following procedures.

INITIATING BANK CLASSIFICATION

Expansion behavior is viewed as a stochastic process governed by
the initiating bank's innate characteristics. Large, well managed
banks generally branch and merge more frequently than small or
unevenly managed ones. Hence, size and managerial qualities of
banks are employed to investigate differences in expansion conduct.
While it is possible that a continuum of initiating behavior exists, it
is assumed that five discrete categories fully characterize expansion
aggressiveness. Each bank in the state can be classified into one of
the five categories. It is assumed that all banks in a particular
category behave in the same way concerning merger initiation.
Similarly, it is assumed that each bank in a class initiates de novo
branch expansion attempts in a manner identical to all other banks
in the same class.

Data for each of 233 banks was analyzed to identify general
categories of expansion behavior. Based on this inspection, each
bank was grouped subjectively into one of five discrete classes. The
characteristics of the banks in these classes were then used to
estimate the equations that classify banks in the simulation. Thus
the equations defined to place banks into expansion initiation
categories are a statistical representation of the author's original
subjective grouping scheme. Five distinct classes are identified and
defined.

Class 1. A potential lead bank of a statewide branch or holding
company system has:

- resources (usually over $400 million in assets) to expand statewide;
- a history of aggressive expansion;
- no management succession problems;
- frequently high quality management.

Class 2. A significant regional competitor bank capable of operating a large branch or holding company system has:

- resources (assets between $150 and $500 million) to expand extensively;
- a history of de novo branching and merging;
- no management succession problems;
- usually high or average quality management.

Class 3. A significant competitor bank in its home market, usually with an important share of the market has:

- assets in the range of $50 to $200 million;
- several offices, usually more than three;
- infrequent management succession problems;
- usually high or average quality management.

Class 4. A locally competitive bank has:

- assets between $15 and $75 million;
- usually between one and four offices;
- fairly frequent succession problems;
- usually competent management.

Class 5. A convenient local depository bank has:

- assets less than $25 million;
- the majority possess one office only;
- a high percentage of management succession problems;
- usually average or low quality management.

Asset size is used to give an indication of a bank's available resources to initiate merger and de novo branch attempts. The number of offices that a bank operates is evidence of its historical aggressiveness in expanding. Management quality and succession problems are employed to measure a bank's ability to expand. The variables actually used are defined below:

C_1, bank assets (log base 10);
C_2, management succession problems (yes = 1, no = 0);
C_3, management quality variable;
C_4, management quality variable;
C_5, number of branches (log base 10).

Problems in estimating the multiple discriminant and classification equations derive from two sources. First, the five groups are somewhat arbitrarily specified.[2] There are undoubtedly several broad categories of expansion activity among banks—perhaps a very large number of such groups. However, it is felt that five classes of homogeneous banks capture sufficient diversity in expansion behavior while remaining a manageably small number. The groups are exhaustive and mutually exclusive.

Another source of problems in classifying banks concerns the nature of variables C_2, C_3, and C_4. These are each zero-one variables based upon estimates of management quality and potential succession problems obtained from bank examination data. All examinations were in the November 1970 to November 1971 time period. It is assumed that neither management quality nor the succession status of a bank alters during the course of the simulation.

Management succession (problem versus no problem) is a subjective judgment based upon the examiner's opinion, ages of top- and middle-level management, and salary scales. The management succession variable assumes a value of one if there is a problem, zero otherwise. Management quality is estimated as high, average, or low relative to other banks of a similar size and location. In quantifying this variable, the opinion of the bank examiner was of primary importance. The management quality variables operate in the following fashion:

$$\left.\begin{array}{l} C_3 = 1 \\ C_4 = 0 \end{array}\right\} \text{high quality management;}$$

$$\left.\begin{array}{l} C_3 = 0 \\ C_4 = 0 \end{array}\right\} \text{average quality management;}$$

$C_3 = 0$
$C_4 = 1$ } low quality management.

Discriminant equations are estimated from the 233 subjectively grouped banks. Since a combination of continuous and discrete variables is employed, a quadratic reduced space technique is utilized for classification. A logarithmic transformation of variables C_1 and C_5 yields superior results in reclassifying banks, probably by reducing extreme skewness in the data. The results obtained by running the original 233 observations through the estimated equations and classifying them into groups appear below.

	Class	Predicted Class Membership				
		1	2	3	4	5
Actual Class	1	6	0	0	0	0
Membership	2	0	5	0	0	0
	3	0	1	9	0	0
	4	0	0	0	56	3
	5	0	0	0	11	136

Overall, 212 of the original 233 observations (over 90%) are correctly classified by the estimated equations and classification rules. Entries along the array's main diagonal represent agreement between the original subjective classification and the statistical classification procedure. Other entries denote improper classifications by the estimated equations. For example, the row 3, column 2 observation denotes a bank subjectively placed in class 3 that the discriminant equations place in class 2. Further examination of other misclassified observations reveals two important aspects of the procedure's operation. First, no bank is displaced more than one class in error. For example, all misclassified class 4 banks are placed in class 3 or class 5. Second, the majority of classification errors occur in the smaller size categories where class distinctions are less definite. Both these factors mitigate the potential impact of classification errors within the simulation.

The discriminant equations are used in the simulation to reclassify a bank into one of the five groups following each merger or de novo branch accomplished by that bank. It is assumed that banks in each class maintain a constant relative likelihood of initiating an expansion attempt vis-à-vis banks of other classes. This is defined as a constant and innate characteristic of each class bank.

The relative likelihoods are estimated from the behavior of Pennsylvania banks in the 1970/71 period. Explicitly, in this time period each class 1 bank was approximately 15% more likely to initiate a merger attempt than a class 2 bank, etc. The following are the likelihood measures utilized in the simulation. Each likelihood measure is for the class bank relative to the next lower class bank.

Class	Number of Merger Attempts	Approximate Number of Banks	Merger/ Bank	Relative Likelihood
1	11	15	0.733	1.15
2	14	22	0.636	4.29
3	4	27	0.148	2.75
4	7	130	0.054	14.38
5	1	267	0.0037	

Similar likelihoods are estimated from the same period for de novo branching attempts.

Class	Number of Branch Attempts	Approximate Number of Banks	Branch/ Bank	Relative Likelihood
1	65	15	4.33	3.39
2	28	22	1.27	2.15
3	16	27	0.592	1.38
4	56	130	0.430	5.06
5	23	267	0.085	

The probability of a bank initiating a merger or branch attempt is determined in the simulation by resolving a system of simultaneous equations (separate systems for de novo branches and mergers). For example, the merger initiation equations appear below, the unknowns are the Ps.

$$N_1P_1 + N_2P_2 + N_3P_3 + N_4P_4 + N_5P_5 = 1.00$$
$$P_1 = 1.15P_2$$
$$P_2 = 4.29P_3l$$
$$P_3 = 2.75P_4$$
$$P_4 = 14.38P_5$$

where

P_i: probability of an ith class initiating a merger;
N_i: current number of banks in the ith class.

Only the relative likelihoods remain constant throughout the simulation. As the number of banks (N_i) in each class changes, the P_i for all banks are adjusted so that the cumulative probability sums to unity. Each bank in a class has the same initiation probability. In the monte carlo procedures employed in the simulation, the P_i determine the probability of a bank being selected to initiate a merger. The de novo branch initiation equations operate in a similar fashion.

Several law-specific operating rules are also defined for use in the simulation. These rules are introduced primarily for operational reasons. Certain fairly weak class-specific behavioral constraints greatly reduce the processing time necessary for simulation runs. These additional constraints probably do not significantly alter the simulation results. However, they should be considered when evaluating the outcomes of various simulation experiments. Note that specific bank class restrictions are completely arbitrary and are not inclusions in any actual law. In addition, no behavioral constraints are defined for the contiguous county law since the expansion choice sets are sufficiently limited.

The statewide law allows class 1 and class 2 banks to de novo branch anywhere in the state. For these banks, mergers initiated with class 1 to class 4 banks anywhere in the state and class 5 banks within 75 miles are feasible. Class 3 banks can de novo branch in home office or contiguous markets only. Mergers by class 3 banks can be initiated with banks within 75 miles. All initiating activity by class 4 and class 5 banks must be within the home office or contiguous markets.

The holding company law allows only class 1 and class 2 banks to form holding companies. Class 1 banks can search statewide for holding company acquisitions; class 2 banks are restricted to their lead bank district. It is assumed that holding company lead banks always merge where legally feasible and make holding company acquisitions elsewhere.

Under the district law, class 1 and class 2 banks are allowed to de novo branch and initiate mergers districtwide or in formerly allowable areas. Class 3 banks can initiate mergers with same district banks or previously available banks within 75 miles of their home office. De novo branching is allowed for class 3 banks only within the home office or adjacent markets in legally available areas. Class 4 and class 5 banks can initiate expansion attempts only within the home office or contiguous markets in counties legally open.

In summary, all banks are classified into five discrete behavioral classes by the discriminant model. Class membership determines the frequency of expansion initiation and the geographical regions that can be searched for acquisition candidates and markets for new offices. Following each acquisition and de novo branch opening, the initiating bank is reclassified. If the expansion causes the initiating bank to grow sufficiently large, it is placed into a new behavioral class. Otherwise, it remains in its original category. After class placement of the initiating bank, the two systems of simultaneous equations that compute initiation probabilities are resolved to account for the possible class change of the initiator and the disappearance of a bank if an acquisition transpired. Thus class membership and initiation probabilities are continuously updated.

BANK MERGERS

There are several economic incentives that encourage bank mergers. One important merger motivation derives from the maximization of firm valuation. An acquisition can provide an outlet for the initiating bank to expand its loan and deposit opportunities while simultaneously diversifying its asset and liability portfolios. In addition, an inefficiently managed bank with established customer relations can represent an attractive investment to an aggressive bank that has the resources to upgrade the acquired bank's personnel. In either case, the two banks operating together are more efficient than the independent organizations. As a result, the stockholder groups of both banks benefit from the merger.

The procedure used to model the simulation's bank combination process incorporates the essential aspects of actual merger behavior. The objective is to accurately describe the entire merger environment so that generally applicable behavioral equations can be estimated. The first step is to define a variety of screening and data transformation techniques that mitigate the influence of existing legal and regulatory instruments on observed expansion activity. These procedures are undertaken to assure that the merger equations operate reasonably under each of the various legal and regulatory regimes detailed in previous chapters. The second step is to define a large number of bank and market characteristics that measure the opportunities available through expansion activity. Consultations with several bank executives from banks that are active expansion initiators aided in the choice of particular variables. These bankers represent a wide variety of commercial banks —a large Philadelphia bank, two medium-sized metropolitan banks outside Philadelphia, a very active smaller bank, and a small rural bank. The opinions of these bankers concerning the steps in partner selection and important variables were reassuringly uniform.

A synthesis of the information obtained from interviews and previous studies results in the assumptions, procedures, and variables incorporated in the model.[3] Briefly, the model comprises several screens for eliminating infeasible partners. When the final choice set is specified, a decision rule picks a unique merger partner from the set of potential candidates. All banks in the state are separated into two sets for each merger attempt. Only banks legally available, likely to meet regulatory approval, and not larger than the initiator are considered potential partners. The remainder are excluded from the analysis. The screening procedures are designed to serve several purposes. First, eliminating banks that state law and perceived regulatory policy render unavailable for acquisition recreates as closely as possible the actual choice sets that confront observed intiators. Second, when coupled with an appropriate data transformation outlined below, the screens help eliminate biases in observed partner choice introduced by existing law and policy. Third, the screens, especially the rule that eliminates banks larger than the initiator, serve to reduce the number of potential partners that must be evaluated in the simulation. This speeds the simulation of each legal-regulatory experiment and allows more extensive testing of alternative structural control instruments.

When a bank is chosen to initiate a merger attempt in the simulation, it must search for a suitable combination partner. In an effort to duplicate the actual merger process, an analysis of all known bank merger attempts in the Third Federal Reserve District between 1968 and 1971 (inclusive) was conducted. A total of 48 merger attempts were identified and used. To simplify the analysis, only mergers between two banks are included. (There were two mergers comprising three banks during the period considered.)

In analyzing the historical merger cases, the set of potential partners is further subdivided. One subset contains the single bank actually chosen as a partner. The other subset consists of potentially available banks that satisfy all criteria (as outlined above) vis-à-vis the specific initiator but were not chosen. These subsets are then separately aggregated over all choice situations. The final "chosen" subset contains 48 observations; the "unchosen" subset contains 1,759 observations. A major problem in the specification of these sets exists because they are not mutually exclusive. The division of potential candidate banks on the basis of chosen versus unchosen is not a completely accurate separation of attractive and unattractive merger choices. Many unchosen but fully available and ostensibly attractive potential merger partners remain independent at any particular time because, in general, only one bank may be selected per merger attempt. A short time later, these banks may enter the chosen set in some comparable choice situation. Conversely, such banks may remain unchosen because of characteristics not easily observable or quantifiable. Other banks are actively pursued for equally unobservable reasons. Consequently, there exists considerable overlap between the two sets with resultant problems in analysis.[4] The sets are discrete and exhaustive.

Four primary assumptions are incorporated into the model. The first concerns the operable state law. It is assumed that bankers are completely informed of the provisions of any law governing bank mergers and instantly become cognizant of changes in the law. The state law is the first screen separating feasible from infeasible merger partners. Those banks that are proscribed from combining with the specific initiator are not considered feasible merger candidates.

A second assumption concerns the interaction between partner choice and regulatory policy. It is postulated that banks perceive the currently operable regulatory policy and do not consider partners whom they deem unlikely to meet regulatory approval. Current regulatory policy is expressed as an equation dependent upon the joint characteristics of the initiating bank and its feasible partner. This equation represents the regulatory policy perceived by initiating banks (with a small difference detailed below). Using this equation as a screen, certain legally feasible banks that would create a combination unacceptable to the regulatory agencies are eliminated from the choice set. The banks remaining after these screening procedures are termed potential partners.

The method employed in estimating the regulatory functions are detailed in Chapter V. In analyzing actual merger attempts, the historical policy-regulatory equation is used to represent initiating banks' perceptions of operable regulatory policy. The sole difference between the regulator's own decision rule and the merger initiator's screen equation rests in each group's a priori probability of merger approval. Initiators are assumed to be more optimistic with respect to favorable regulatory action (expressed as a higher a priori probability of approval) than the regulators. The divergence between a priori approval probabilities explains why some attempted mergers are denied by the regulatory agencies. The initiator's a priori approval probability is fixed at 0.90.

The third major assumption specifies that only banks of equal or smaller deposit size than the initiators are considered behaviorally feasible partners. This assumption is used for several reasons. It is unlikely on theoretical grounds that a bank would possess the resources necessary to absorb a bank larger than itself. Moreover, no case among the 48 studied involved such an occurrence. In addition, this assumption streamlines the choice procedure by quickly eliminating a large number of banks in each merger situation. Certain other behavioral constraints relating to distances searched for potential partners are detailed in the initiator classification section of this chapter.

The fourth assumption in this study asserts that attractive partners can be identified on the basis of each candidate bank's characteristics relative to other potential partners and the initiating bank. Thus relative characteristic magnitudes rather than the absolute values of particular variables are important for merger partner choice. This assumption is necessitated by the provisions of the present Pennsylvania state law that segments potential partner choice sets. While initiator banks throughout the state manage to find merger partners, the banks available for merging are a decidedly nonhomogeneous group differing in size and market characteristics from region to region. This means that the distributions of several characteristics are nonstationary across choice sets. To allow aggregation of individual merger data obtained from combinations observed throughout the state, several variables must be transformed to place all characteristic values on a comparable scale. The transformation operates by mapping each relevant characteristic into two zero-one dummy variables. For example, for each potential partner in a given choice set, the jth characteristic (M_J) is replaced by (M_{JA}) and (M_{JB}). Then the following rule is applied.

$M_{JA} = 1$
$M_{JB} = 0$ if M_J is among the largest ⅓ values of M_J relative to other potential partners in the given choice set.

$M_{JA} = 0$
$M_{JB} = 0$ if M_J is among the middle ⅓ values of M_J relative to other potential partners in the given choice set.

$M_{JA} = 0$
$M_{JB} = 1$ if M_J is among the smallest ⅓ values of M_J relative to other potential partners in the given choice set.

This transformation generates homogeneous observations in all merger choice situations. Hence, one estimating procedure can be applied to mergers that occurred in different parts of the state.

As another attractive property, the transformation also frees the estimated merger partner selection process from the influence of current regulatory policy and state law. The existing structural control instruments place certain banks out of bounds for each initiator. With an alternative regulatory-legal arrangement, these banks become potential partners. In such circumstances, the distributions of partner characteristics could be significantly altered. The transformation detailed above eliminates this possibility. Thus the resultant choice procedures are generally applicable under different state law and regulatory policy specifications.

In defining characteristics to describe a potential partner's market envrionment, a concentration measure is one important parameter. The concentration variable employed in this study is the numbers-equivalent (G).[5] This measure is derived from the thermodynamic measure of entropy (H), the amount of disorder existing in a system. In the context of industrial organization, (H) quantifies the degree of uncertainty confronting market competitors in evaluating the banking choice of a potential customer. At one extreme, if all banks in a local market are equal-sized, then each firm is, on average, equally likely to attract a potential customer. This represents maximum uncertainty and maximum entropy. Conversely, great size disparity among banks means there is less uncertainty concerning customer choice. That is, large banks tend to attract more customers than small banks. At this exteme, a monopoly bank faces no uncertainty concerning the banking choice of the potential customer. If it is assumed that equal-sized firms create maximum competition for a given number of banks and a monopoly bank generates minimum competition, then entropy and competition are monotonically related.

The entropy of market j is calculated in the following fashion:

$$(6) \qquad H_j = - \sum_{i=1}^{N_j} X_{ij} \log_2 X_{ij} \; ;$$

where X_{ij} = the ith bank's share of total deposits in market j;

N_j = the number of banks operating in market j.

A local market's numbers-equivalent (G) is obtained directly from (H). (G_j) indicates the number of equal-sized banks that generate the same level of competition existing with the actual number and size distribution of banks in the jth market. The numbers-equivalent is simply

$$(7) \qquad G_j = \text{antilog } H_j .$$

A local market's numbers-equivalent can vary between 1 and N_j. If all N_j banks in local market j are equal-sized, $G_j = N_j$. Conversely, if $N_j = 5$ and one bank controls 90% of market deposits while the remaining four banks equally share 10%, then $G_j = 1.6$. Obviously, a near monopoly exists in this situation.

The numbers-equivalent is a superior concentration measure for several reasons. First, it is based upon a definite theory of competition. Explicitly, competition among firms is viewed as each oranization's ability to attract random customers in the market. Second, (G) utilizes information from the entire size distribution of competitors in a market rather than focusing on some few major enterprises like a concentration ratio. Third, the numbers-equivalent is measured on a readily interpreted scale. Monopoly equals unity and maximum competition equals (N).

The variables included for the merger partner analysis are divided into four general categories. *Partner-specific* variables attempt to measure certain characteristics of a potential partner bank and its management that might be pertinent in considering it as a merger partner. *Market resource* variables are designed to indicate whether the market of the potential partner is attractive for entry and growth. *Competition* variables are included as another dimension of the candidate bank's environment. *Joint* variables attempt to capture the information and control problems an initiator might confront in seeking or combining with a specific partner.

Partner-Specific Characteristics

M_1: Bank is a member of the Federal Reserve System.
(Yes = 1, No = 0)

M_2: Bank has a management succession problem.
(Yes = 1, No = 0)

M_3: Number of offices of bank.

M_4: Deposit size of bank.

M_5: Candidate has initiated a de novo branch or merger in the past two years.
(Yes = 1, No = 0)

Market Resource Variables

M_6: Number of manufacturing establishments in candidate's home office market (1970 data).

M_7: Deposits per office in candidate bank's home office market.

M_8: Population per office in candidate's home office market (1970 data).

Competition Variables

M_9: Number of banking offices in the candidate's home office market.

M_{10}: Numbers-equivalent of candiate's home office markets.

Joint Characteristics

M_{11}: Distance between home office of initiator and candidate.

M_{12}: Candidate's home office is in initiator's home office market. (Yes $=$ 1, No $=$ 0)

M_{13}: Initiator is among the smallest 1/2 banks in its home office market and candidate is in initiator's home office market. (Yes $=$ 1, No $=$ 0)

To allow aggregation across choice sets, all relevant variables are transformed into one-zero dummy variables on the basis of the transformation detailed previously. (It is not necessary to transform variables M_1, M_2, M_5, M_{12}, or M_{13}.)

The specification of the a priori probability of attractiveness creates a major conceptual problem. While only about 3% of all potential partners were selected, this reflects the nature of the merger process rather than the number of attractive merger partners. Explicitly, once a bank is included in the potential partner set there is no a priori reason for assuming it is not attractive. The overlapping nature of the chosen and unchosen subsets causes the problem. That is, the 48 chosen banks were not the only attractive merger partners available. Following discussions with bankers and regulators, it was determined somewhat arbitrarily that a third of the potential partner banks are attractive partners at any given time.

Extensive experimentation was conducted with two discriminant analysis procedures. Since all variables can assume only discrete zero-one values, a linear reduced space technique and a quadratic reduced space procedure were investigated (see this chapter's appendix). The best results were obtained with a linear reduced space procedure. The discriminant equation and classification statistics are presented on the following page.

An F test of the null hypothesis of group mean vector equality yields $F = 7.65425$ with 15 and 1,971 degrees of freedom. This allows rejection of the null hypothesis at the .01 significance level.

The table below indicates classification results.

	Predicted Attractive Group	Predicted Unattractive Group
Actual Chosen Group	25	23
Actual Unchosen Group	150	1609

Thus 25 of the 48 actual partners (52%) are properly categorized as attractive. In addition, 1609 of 1759 (91%) of the unchosen banks are correctly classed as unattractive.

While a significant amount of discriminating power is obtained, the classification equation is less powerful than is desirable.[6] The difficulty arises from two sources. The first concerns the initial specification of group membership. The criterion of entering versus not entering a merger is not a completely adequate method for separating attractive from unattractive banks. Second, the available variables do not provide enough descriptive power of banks and their environment, particularly after transformation. The decision rule adopted for initiators to select particular merger partners in the simulation flows from the estimated discriminant equation and classification rule. For each initiator, the potential partner with the highest probability ($\geqslant.5$) of "attractive group" membership as calculated with the classification equation is specified the chosen bank. No consideration of whether the chosen bank would agree to merge is included.

Overall, the results of the merger partner selection procedure are less than perfect, but they are still quite useful. The various screens insure that unreasonable pairings will not occur. The final decision

Merger Partner Choice Equation

Variable	Discriminant Equation Coefficient ($\underline{V}$)	Percent Discriminating Power
M1	0.0028	0.1610
M2	0.0580	3.1649
M3A	− 0.1125	6.5200
M3B	− 0.1608	9.2660
M4A	0.0622	3.6003
M4B	− 0.0712	4.1203
M5	− 0.0934	4.3621
M6A	− 0.1968	11.4048
M6B	− 0.0118	0.6842
M7A	− 0.1179	6.8313
M7B	− 0.0095	0.5496
M8A	− 0.0162	0.9379
M8B	− 0.0231	1.3383
M9A	0.1727	10.0021
M9B	− 0.0184	1.0652
M10A	− 0.1007	5.8341
M10B	− 0.0237	1.3721
M11A	− 0.0136	0.7842
M11B	0.0631	3.6368
M12	0.4193	16.6161
M13	0.8160	7.7489

Classification statistics: Reduced Space Means

$$CA = 0.2109$$
$$CU = -0.1438$$

Reduced Space Variance
$$D = 0.0401$$

rule provides some measure of confidence that "attractive" partners will be chosen a large percentage of the time. Obviously, more work in this area is necessary.

SELECTION OF MARKETS FOR NEW BRANCHES

Banks chosen to be expansion initiators are also allowed the option of de novo branching in the simulation. De novo branching is treated in a manner analogous to merging. The initiating bank must identify the legally available set of markets and choose the most attractive one from the feasible alternatives. However, no regulatory screen is employed in the branching procedure. Extensive analysis directed toward identifying a de novo branch regulatory rule was unsuccessful with the variables utilized. In addition, no general behavioral restrictions are applied to de novo branch initiators in the analysis of actual new branch initiatives. Specific well defined class restrictions on the extent of market search under alternative legal environments are covered in the initiator classification section of this chapter.

All de novo branch applications in Pennsylvania for the period 1968/1971 were analyzed to investigate the characteristics of attractive de novo branching markets. A total of 375 observations of chosen markets were obtained. Problems similar to those present in the merger analysis were encountered. Explicitly, many markets enter different subsets in comparable choice situations. Virtually every market in the state was chosen at least once during the period investigated. At the same time, virtually every market was not chosen several times in an apparently comparable situation. Consequently, there is considerable overlap between the chosen and unchosen market subsets. However, in branch market choice, frequency of selection provides additional information that is not available in the merger analysis.

A list of legally feasible markets was constructed for banks headquartered in each county. The number of available alternatives ranges between 3 and 14 markets, depending on the county's location. For each choice situation, the set of feasible markets is divided into two subsets—the chosen market and the unchosen markets. These subsets are separately aggregated over all choice situations examined, yielding a subset of 375 chosen markets and 2,043 observations in the unchosen subset. Discriminant analysis and classification techniques are employed with these groups to identify the characteristics of attractive versus unattractive markets. The basic assumption is that chosen markets are more attractive than unchosen markets.

The variables employed to gauge the branching potential of a market are listed below. Many of the same variables are used in both the merger partner and de novo branch analyses. This reflects the assumpton that merging and branching are essentially expansion substitutes. As in the merger study, the variables may be divided into general categories measuring different dimensions of the market. *Market resource* variables are employed to measure the commercial potential of a market. The *competitive measure* variables are included to reflect the competition an additional entry into a market might confront from established enterprises. The *joint initiator-market* variable is designed to capture the behavior smaller banks might display in attempting wider expansion. That is, information gathering is less difficult when evaluating the home office market.

Market Resource Variables

Y_1: Market population (1970).
Y_2: Number of manufacturing establishments in the market (1970).
Y_3: Deposits per office in the market.
Y_4: Deposit growth rate in market (1968/1971).
Y_5: Market population per office.

Competitive Measure Variables

Y_6: Number of banking offices in the market.
Y_7: Numbers-equivalent of the market.
Y_8: Number of banks larger than initiator in the market.
Y_9: Number of banks smaller than initiator in the market.

Joint Initiator-Market Variable

Y_{10}: Initiator is among smallest $\frac{1}{2}$ banks in its home office market and market considered is its home office market.
(Yes = 1, No = 0)

Problems similar to those encountered in the merger study are confronted in the process of aggregating the chosen and unchosen subsets. There exists tremendous diversity among the feasible choice sets available to various banks because the existing law creates partitioned choice sets. At the same time, branching activity persists in virtually every portion of the state. Consequently, all variables are transformed to rank each market's characteristics relative to the other feasible alternatives in each choice set. This places all markets on a comparable basis that allows aggregation.

De Novo Branch Market Choice Equation

Variable	Discrimanant Equation Coefficients (Y)	Percent Discriminating Power
Y1A	0.0482	2.4322
Y1B	− 0.1215	6.3022
Y2A	0.0592	2.9670
Y2B	0.0467	2.4162
Y3A	− 0.0958	4.8522
Y3B	0.0522	2.6959
Y4A	0.0157	0.8221
Y4B	− 0.0669	3.4723
Y5A	− 0.0756	3.9118
Y5B	0.0793	4.1219
Y6A	− 0.0978	4.9044
Y6B	0.1268	6.5837
Y7A	− 0.0724	3.7261
Y7B	0.0334	1.7385
Y8A	− 0.1562	7.7506
Y8B	− 0.1627	8.5586
Y9A	− 0.2060	3.3268
Y9B	− 0.0636	3.9118
Y10	− 0.9051	19.1716

Classification Statistics: Reduced Space Means

$$CA = -0.6150$$
$$CU = -0.1873$$

Reduced Space Variances

$$DA = 0.1477$$
$$DU = 0.0409$$

The transformation employed is identical to that specified in the merger analysis. Variable Y_{10} is not transformed.

The a priori probability of market attractiveness poses a problem in the de novo branch analysis. Overall, about 12% of the total observations are chosen markets. However, this reflects the nature of the branching process and the construction of the choice subsets. There is no a priori reason for any legally feasible market to be unchosen. However, discussions with several bankers indicated that approximately half the markets available at any given time may be considered attractive enough to encourage de novo branching. On this basis, the a priori probability of market attractiveness is specified as one half.

Linear and quadratic discriminant procedures were tested on the transformed data. The best results are obtained with the quadratic reduced space methods. (See this chapter's appendix.) An F test of the null hypothesis—group mean vector equality—yielded F = 52.75 with 19 and 2,398 degrees of freedom. This allows rejection of the null hypothesis at a .01 level of significance.

Classification results are indicated in the table.

	Predicted Attractive Market	Predicted Unattractive Market
Actual Chosen Market	224	151
Actual Unchosen Market	213	1,830

About 60% of the actually chosen markets are properly classified attractive while 89% of the unchosen markets are categorized unattractive.

The decision rule adopted for de novo branch market selection employs the estimated discriminant equation to calculate probabilities of group membership. The available market with the highest ($\geqslant .5$) probability of being an attractive market is specified as the chosen alternative. This choice procedure possesses an inherent shortcoming for use in a simulation. If the rule is employed without modification, it implies that banks will repeatedly choose the same market while it remains most attractive. Actually, bank behavior is seldom this uniform. While most expansion activity may focus on one market, some de novo branching usually occurs in other markets as well. In an effort to duplicate this behavior, a weighted choice procedure is adopted. As an arbitrary rule, choice is limited to the three markets with highest probability of inclusion in the attractive set. The selection procedure is as follows:

Let: Pr_i = probability i^{th} market is an attractive set,
   $i = 1, 2, 3$. $\text{Pr}_i \geqslant 0.5$ for all i.

$$Q_i = \frac{\text{Pr}_i}{\text{Pr1} + \text{Pr2} + \text{Pr3}}$$

Markets are randomly chosen with probability Q_i. Hence, a market that ranks high relative to the other two markets is selected more frequently. Conversely, if all three markets have approximately the same probability of entering the attractive set, they each are chosen nearly as frequently. In most situations, several markets have $\text{Pr} \geqslant$

0.5. This means an initiating bank may branch into several markets during the same time period.

ELAPSED TIME ACCOUNTING

An elapsed time accounting procedure is used to place the simulation in annual format and to order the branch and merge decisions. It rests on three basic assumptions. First, the banking system is expansion-oriented and will remain so. Second, the state banking system, as a whole, has some maximum yearly expansion ability. Third, it is postulated that the annual expansion capacity is a function of the number of banks. These conditions oversimplify the expansion process but the relationships are useful in operating the simulation.

It is hypothesized that the number of mergers is directly related to the number of banks while the amount of de novo branch activity is inversely related to the number of banks. That is, as the number of potential merger partners diminishes, less merging occurs while greater branching activity becomes manifest. As an initial approximation, simple linear functions are adopted to model overall annual statewide expansion activity.

A model using time series data consisting of the number of mergers per year, the number of de novo branches per year, and the number of banks at the beginning of each year in Pennsylvania during the period 1961/1971 inclusive was tested. The best results are obtained by specifying a first order autocorrelation structure. Model:

$$(6) \qquad MG_t = a_o + a_1 BK_t + u_t$$
$$u_t = u_{t-1} + \varepsilon_t$$
$$(7) \qquad BR_t = \beta_o + \beta_1 BK_t + v_t$$
$$v_t = v_{t-1} + \delta_t$$

MG_t : Number of mergers in year t.
BR_t : Number of de novo branches in year t.
BK_t : Number of banks at the beginning of year t.
u,v: Autocorrelated error terms.
Σ, δ: Serially independent error terms.

A Cochrane-Orcutt iterative process is used to independently estimate each equation in the model.[7] For example, with equation (6), the procedure starts with an arbitrary value for ρ, then minimizes the sum of squares. Using the a estimate from this stage, a ρ value is estimated. This ρ is then used to estimate a new value for a. The process is continued until successive estimates of a differ by some arbitrarily small amount. Estimates for a, β, ρ, and λ appear below.

(6a) $MG_t = 19.479 + .751BK_t$
             (4.376)   (9.734)

$\rho = -0.737$

$\bar{R}^2 = .865;\ SE = 2.784;\ DW = 2.280$

(7a) $BR_t = 183.773 - 1.889BK_t$
             (8.306)   (4.908)

$\lambda = -0.458$

$\bar{R}^2 = .571;\ SE = 11.383;\ DW = 1.712$

(t values in parentheses, 8 degrees of freedom)

All variables have the correct signs and all t values are significant at the .01 level. The negative serial correlation may indicate that years of intensive expansion activity are followed by years when some managerial energy is directed toward consolidation of recent gains.

It is possible that the level of expansion activity is constrained by state law that limits banks' regions of feasible expansion. However, some slight evidence indicates that Pennsylvania banks have found sufficient outlets for their expansion efforts to date. Explicitly, large Philadelphia banks have only recently begun moving their home office designations to Montgomery County. Under the present contiguous county branching and merging law, this movement opens additional markets to expansion while deleting none of the possible markets from Philadelphia County. These banks are among the most expansion-initiating organizations in the state. If their activity had not been constrained in the past, it is likely that earlier movement would have been evidenced. This partially supports the hypothesis that the above equations measure the Pennsylvania banking system's annual unconstrained expansion propensity.

With equations (6a) and (7a), the expected number of de novo branches and mergers during a year can be predicted given the number of banks at the beginning of the year. Within the simulation, a Guassian random number generator provides values for the error terms. Predicted expansion activity is arrayed in a random sequence of de novo branches and mergers. The initiating bank is then chosen with the class probabilities calculated for the specified type expansion attempt. An *expansion equivalent year* has elapsed when the merger and branch sequence is exhausted. The next year's initial number of banks is calculated by subtracting the number of mergers from the preceding year's beginning number of banks. No allowance is provided for failures and other bank or branch closings in the simulation.[8]

The elapsed time procedure places future expansion behavior on an historical basis. It provides a standard for measuring the impact of regulatory or legal changes on market structure. Explicitly, it is possible that an altered state law or regulatory policy might cause an exogenous increase in expansion activity. A permanent increase in yearly expansion attempts can be simulated by increasing the intercept term in equations (1) and (2). For example, if a 10% rise in annual mergers is projected, the constant term in equation (6a) is increased from 19.479 to 21.427. Alternatively, a changed legal environment might cause an initial spurt in expansion activity followed by gradual reversion to the historical rate. This can be simulated with a two-stage process. The constant terms in equations (6a) and (7a) are first increased by the desired amount. A difference equation then reduces the increased intercepts to their original value through time.

The behavioral relationships modeled in this chapter operate together in the simulation to provide the environment for testing alternative structural control instruments. State law and regulatory policy interact with innate behavior by constraining the acquisition partner and de novo branch choice sets. In turn, the acquisition and branching procedures are designed to operate under a wide variety of control instrument combinations. By repeatedly choosing initiators, matching partner banks or new branch markets with the initiators, and signalling for market data updating, the behavioral relationships drive the simulation under each regulatory-legal specification. After sufficient time elapses for the impact of new policies and laws to be manifest in local banking markets, cumulative results are generated by the simulation program. In Chapter VII, outcomes for regulatory-legal experiments are presented and tested to ascertain the influence of structural control instruments on measures of local market competition.

NOTES

1. The term "structural control agencies" is used to encompass the state legislature, federal regulatory agencies, and the U.S. Justice Department.

2. See Eisenbeis [13] for a discussion of this problem.

3. Cohen and Reid [8], Gilbert [18], and Mullineaux (34).

4. See Eisenbeis and Avery [12] for a discussion of the problems caused by overlapping groups.

5. The following discussion of entropy and the numbers-equivalent is adopted from Horowitz [25].

6. The results obtained may be compared with approximate expected classification resulting from random group assignments:

		Predicted Group	
		1	2
Actual Group	1	16	32
	2	586	1173

7. Johnson [27] pp. 262–265.

8. During the period 1960/1971, only two banks ceased operations in Pennsylvania for reasons other than merger or absorption. Within the same period, 56 branches closed. However, many of these branch closings represent a small change in branch location rather than a total cessation of operation in the given area.

APPENDIX

Reduced Space Classification Procedures*

Where zero-one variables occur in the analysis, a multivariate normal model of the observation vectors' distribution is not neces-

---

*This section is derived entirely from Cooley and Lohnes [9], Chapters 6 and 7, and Eisenbeis and Avery [13].

sarily a good approximation. Reduced space methods rely upon the Central Limit Theorem to assume that linear combinations of random variables are more likely to be normally distributed than the component variates. Briefly, the multiple discriminant equations are employed as linear transformations to map test space values into discriminant or reduced space. It is assumed that the resultant discriminant scores approximate a multivariate normal distribution.

The first step is to obtain the linear discriminant functions. The objective is to maximize the ratio of among groups sums of squares to within groups sums of squares.

Define:

N_G: The number of observations per g^{th} group variable; $n_g = 1 \ldots Ng$.

M: The number of variables; $m = 1 \ldots M$.

G: Number of groups; $g = 1 \ldots G$.

R: The number of discriminant functions; $r = 1 \ldots R$; $R = \min(M, G\text{-}1)$.

A: Weighted among groups deviations sums of squares matrix (MXM).

$$a_{ij} = \sum_{g=1}^{G} N_g (X_{gm.} - \bar{X}_{.m.})\ (\bar{X}_{gh.} - \bar{X}_{.h.}).$$

W: Pooled within groups deviations sums of squares matrix (MXM).

$$W_{ij} = \sum_{g=1}^{G} \sum_{n=1}^{N_g} (X_{gmn_g} - \bar{X}_{gm.})\ (X_{ghn_g} - \bar{X}_{gh.}).$$

The objective function may be expressed as the matrix equation

1) $\quad \text{Max } \lambda = \dfrac{V'AV}{V'WV}; \qquad\qquad\qquad V_{MXR} = (V_1 \ldots, V_R).$

The vectors $\underset{\sim}{V}_r$ associated with maximum λ_r must be obtained where

2)
$$\lambda_r = \frac{\underset{\sim}{V}'_r A \underset{\sim}{V}_r}{\underset{\sim}{V}_r W \underset{\sim}{V}_r} \, .$$

Expression (2) is maximized with respect to $\underset{\sim}{V}_r$ when

3)
$$\frac{\partial \lambda_r}{\partial \underset{\sim}{V}_r} = \frac{[2[(\underset{\sim}{V}'_r W \underset{\sim}{V}_r) \; A \underset{\sim}{V}_r - (\underset{\sim}{V}'_r A \underset{\sim}{V}_r) \; W \underset{\sim}{V}_r]}{(\underset{\sim}{V}'_r W \underset{\sim}{V}_r)^2} = 0.$$

This equation is simplified by substituting λ_r for the equivalent terms:

4)
$$2 A \underset{\sim}{V}_r - 2\lambda_r W \underset{\sim}{V} = 0$$

5)
$$(A - \lambda_r W) \cdot \underset{\sim}{V}_r = 0$$

6)
$$(W^{-1}A - \lambda_r I) \cdot \underset{\sim}{V}_r = 0.$$

Solving the characteristic equation

7)
$$|W^{-1}A - \underset{\sim}{\lambda}I| = 0$$

obtained from the R partial derivatives $\delta\lambda_r/\delta\underset{\sim}{V}_r$ yields the characteristic roots λ_r. The associated eigenvectors $\underset{\sim}{V}_r$ are the multiple discriminant equations. These linear functions are utilized as linear transformations to map values from test space into discriminant space.

The matrix of group centroids in reduced space is obtained from the matrix of variables means $\overline{X}(MXG)$. The gth column of $\overline{X}$ (MXG) is the vector of variable means of the gth group:

8)
$$C_{(RXG)} = V' \cdot \overline{X}_{(MXG)}; \quad C_{(RXG)} = (\underset{\sim}{C}_1, \ldots, \ C_g).$$

The reduced space pooled dispersion matrix is obtained from the test space pooled covariance matrix $(\sum)$:

9)
$$D_{(RXR)} = V'\sum V.$$

For quadratic classification, each gth within group dispersion matrix is transformed.

Each ith observation vector is also mapped into reduced space. This transformation yields the discriminant scores of the individual observation vectors:

10)
$$\underset{\sim}{X}_{R,\,i} = V'\underset{\sim}{X}_{i}.$$

Based on the assumption of multivariate normal discriminant scores, the quadratic form

11)
$$\chi^2_{i(g)} = (\underset{\sim}{X}_{R,\,i} - \underset{\sim}{C}_g)' \cdot D^{-1} \cdot (\underset{\sim}{X}_{R,\,i} - \underset{\sim}{C}_g)$$

has a chi-square distribution. In quadratic classification, the individual within group reduced space dispersion matrices are used to calculate the N_g chi-square values for each group.

Using the G chi-square distributions obtained in expression (11), the probability that the ith observation vector is in the gth group is derived from Baye's theorem. Equation (12) provides the probability of group membership. (Π_g are a priori probabilities.)

12)
$$P_{ig}(g/\underset{\sim}{X}_i) = \frac{\Pi_g}{\sum\limits_{h=1}^{G} \frac{\Pi_h}{|D|} \; 1/2 \; \exp(-1/2\chi^2_{i(g)})}.$$

Quadratic classification utilizes the transformed within group dispersion matrices rather than the common pooled dispersion matrix. The expression then becomes

13)
$$P_{ig}(g/\underset{\sim}{X}_i) = \frac{\Pi_g}{\sum\limits_{h=1}^{G} \frac{\Pi_h}{|D_h|} \; 1/2 \; \exp(-1/2\chi^2_{i(h)})}.$$

The classification rule employed is

    assign $\underset{\sim}{X}_i$ to group g if

14)
$$P_{ig} \geqslant P_{ih}; \; g, \; h = 1 \ldots G; \; g \neq h.$$

Chapter VII

Analysis of Simulation Results

The bank expansion and control models described in preceding chapters are used to simulate the evolution of the Pennsylvania banking industry during the time period 1971/1981 inclusive. The objective of this chapter's analysis is to demonstrate that different combinations of regulatory policies and state laws have a measurable impact on the competitive structure of local banking markets. This issue is important for the following reason. If the alternative regulatory policies and state laws tested in the simulation do not measurably influence local market structure outcomes, then any combination of the instruments investigated is equally effective (or ineffective) in controlling banking industry evolution. In this case, it makes no difference which combination of structural control instruments among those tested is selected. Conversely, if significant differences in the impacts of instruments are identified, the choice among policies and laws is important.

EXPERIMENTAL CONDITIONS IN THE SIMULATION

Each law and regulatory policy combination is simulated several times to generate distributions of local market outcomes. Regulatory-legal alternatives involving the contiguous county and districtwide laws are iterated ten times, holding company and state-wide laws five times. The period 1971/1981 is chosen for several reasons. The 1971 starting date allows inclusion of a year where actual results are available. This makes possible a comparison of simulated 1971 outcomes with actual expansion activity during 1971. Termination in 1981 is specified because it is felt that the initial data do not warrant projections beyond that period.

Analysis of a particular policy-legal alternative's influence is accomplished by holding other external factors constant. Hence, to measure the effect of one combination of structural control instruments, other laws, regulatory policies, learning rates, and expansion intensities are prespecified and maintained during the experiment. The results presented below are generated with the following fixed conditions. An "historical" regulatory policy is assumed for 1971 and 1972. Any new policy becomes operative in 1973 and for all following years. The learning rate is arbitrarily specified with (a) = 0.90 (see Chapter V). This implies that the banking industry accurately perceives an altered regulatory policy after about 15 merger attempts. Maintenance of historical rates of de novo branching and merging is assumed to occcur following a legal or regulatory change with no transitory jump in activity. Finally, legal alternatives other than the contiguous county law become operative in 1974.

Testing the model's "reasonableness" is accomplished by comparing 1971 simulated behavior with 1971 actual behavior. The results of one simulation run may be found in this chapter's appendix. While the class distribution of simulated expansion initiators in a given iteration deviates somewhat from the class distribution of actual initiators, this merely reflects the random initiator selection process. The average simulated behavior over several runs approaches reality very closely.

The merger partners chosen in the simulation appear quite reasonable in both size and market location. Note that the one actual initiating bank specified its actual partner. Simulated branching patterns also appear to match fairly closely the actual chosen markets. Overall, analysis of several 1971 simulated sequences gives qualitative assurance that the initiator specification, partner and market selection, and regulatory functions operate with an acceptable degree of accuracy.

In assessing simulation projections, it is assumed that measures of local market structure reflect the competitive conduct of the organizations operating in the market. Several summary statistics are adopted to describe predicted market structures. No single measure completely captures the diverse factors that comprise the competitive environment. However, a combination of complementary measures provides a composite description of the individual banking markets. The first summary statistic employed is the numbers-equivalent (G). The three-bank concentration ratio (CR3) is used to impart additional information concerning the largest banks. This statistic is calculated by computing the percent of total market deposits accounted for by the three largest banks operating in each market. In addition, the number of market competitors and total number of offices in the market are used as descriptive statistics. The number of commercial banks operating in the market indicates the number of alternatives available to banking customers. The number of offices measures the convenience aspect of customer service.

A particular strength of this type study derives from the decision maker's ability to identify and monitor markets of particular interest across policy changes. For example, Table 7.1 contains mean results for a selected cross section of markets. Two each of the primary market categories (major urban, other metropolitan, and rural) are included. Column one contains the specified statistics for January 1, 1971. The remaining four columns contain the corresponding mean values for January 1, 1982 produced by simulating the four laws with a fixed "actual" regulatory policy.

The relevant comparisons are among the various laws and predicted 1982 outcomes. In each case, a net decrease of about 140 banks is manifest statewide. However, note that local competition —as measured by the four summary statistics—appears to increase as more liberal laws become operative. In general, structure tends to change most in the smaller markets while the larger established banks maintain their relative positions in the urban markets.

Table 7.1.

Selected Markets	1971 Starting Statistics	Contiguous County	1982 Two-District	Holding Companies	Statewide Branching
Philadelphia:					
Number of banks	27	29	42	32	48
Numbers-equivalent	9.5	8.8	9.1	8.6	9.2
3-Bank concentration ratio	.55	.54	.55	.56	.54
Number of offices	521	776	714	665	697
Pittsburgh:					
Number of banks	39	38	45	53	57
Numbers-equivalent	5.3	5.0	5.4	5.6	5.6
3-Bank concentration ratio	.80	.81	.80	.79	.79
Number of offices	345	492	472	443	473
Harrisburg:					
Number of banks	14	18	21	27	23
Numbers-equivalent	7.0	7.2	7.7	8.9	7.8
3-Bank concentration ratio	.68	.68	.67	.64	.67
Number of offices	54	75	74	94	74
Reading:					
Number of banks	17	30	33	40	37
Numbers-equivalent	7.5	8.6	8.9	11.2	9.4
3-Bank concentration ratio	.72	.70	.70	.64	.68
Number of offices	67	114	100	133	101
Bedford:					
Number of banks	8	12	15	11	16
Numbers-equivalent	6.8	9.1	10.8	8.4	11.5
3-Bank concentration ratio	.63	.55	.50	.51	.51
Number of offices	13	21	25	26	26
Millersburg-Lykens:					
Number of banks	10	19	23	19	23
Numbers-equivalent	8.7	15.0	18.2	14.1	18.3
3-Bank concentration ratio	.54	.40	.36	.41	.36
Number of offices	15	30	34	35	33

A STATISTICAL ANALYSIS OF INDIVIDUAL MARKET OUTCOMES

A two-way analysis of variance technique is used to statistically analyze the simulation's local market projections under different regulatory-legal specifications. The objective is to discover if the structural control instruments measurably influence competitive outcomes in each local banking market. For this purpose, the simulation-generated distributions of each summary statistic in each market are compared under the various laws and regulatory policies. A two-way analysis is undertaken to investigate the independent and joint impacts of alternative structural control instruments.

As an example of the approach employed, suppose the numbers-equivalent measure in each market is the subject of scrutiny. Then each market is analyzed in the following manner. Two treatment categories are investigated, regulatory policy and state law. For each kth local market, an array of outcomes can be constructed.

Numbers-Equivalent Market k

	Potential Competition Policy (P)	Actual Competition Policy (A)	Historical Policy (H)
Statewide Law (SW)	G_{11}	G_{12}	G_{13}
Holding Company Law (HC)	G_{21}	G_{22}	G_{23}
Districtwide Law (DW)	G_{31}	G_{32}	G_{33}
Contiguous County Law (CC)	G_{41}	G_{42}	G_{43}

where G_{ij}: A vector of observed outcomes under law i and policy j. The vector contains observations from the simulation runs.

$i = 1...4; j = 1,2,3.$

The two-way analysis of variance model is specified as:[1]

(1) $$G_{ijr} = u + x_i + \beta_j + \gamma_{ij} + e_{ijr};$$

Where G_{ijr}: the rth observed numbers-equivalent outcome with law i and policy j; $r = 1 \ldots n_{ij}$;

u: the grand mean;

α_i: the effect of the ith law on market k's numbers-equivalent; $\sum_i \alpha_i = 0$;

β_j: the effect of the jth policy on market k's numbers-equivalent; $\sum_j \beta_j = 0$;

γ_{ij}: the joint effect of law i and policy j on the numbers-equivalent in market k; $\sum_i \sum_4 \gamma_{ij} = 0$.

e_{ijr}: a random variable with mean 0 and variance σ^2.

The null hypotheses to be tested are

(i) the α_i all equal zero;
(ii) the β_j all equal zero;
(iii) the γ_{ij} all equal zero.

If the null hypotheses cannot be rejected for market k, it implies that neither state law nor regulatory policy nor the joint effect of the two instruments significantly influences market k's numbers-equivalent measure. Conversely, if any null hypothesis can be rejected, it implies that the corresponding instrument or combination of instruments has a significant influence on market k's projected numbers-equivalent.

The null hypotheses are tested by decomposing the total variability of the observed numbers-equivalent outcomes in market k into terms that can be attributed to the influence of laws, policies, joint effects, and random error.

(2) Total variability = variability due to state law (SSL) +

variability due to regulatory policy (SSP) +

variability due to joint effects (SSI) +
variability due to random error (SSE).

The test statistic for the null hypothesis of no legal influence or $\alpha_i = 0$ is

(3)
$$FL = \frac{SSL/3}{SSE/(N - 12)} \; ;$$

where N: the total number of observations in market k, or

$$\sum_i \sum_{j\cdot} n_{ij} \; .$$

Similarly, the test statistics for regulatory policy (β_j) and joint effects (γ_{ij}) are

(4)
$$FP = \frac{SSP/2}{SSE/(N - 12)}$$

(5)
$$FI = \frac{SSI/6}{SSE/(N-12)} \, .$$

Under the null hypotheses of zero legal, policy, or joint impacts, FL, FP, and FI are values assumed by random variables having F distributions with appropriate degrees of freedom. For example, FP is the value of an F distributed random variable with 2 and (N-12) degrees of freedom.

An identical analysis is conducted for the numbers-equivalent results in each of the 55 local banking markets (Table 7.2). In addition, an analogous framework is used to analyze the results in each market for the projections concerning the number of banks (Table 7.3), the number of branches (Table 7.4), and the three-bank concentration ratio (Table 7.5). Note that the concentration ratio (CR3) is transformed to (1–CR3) to render the measure positively associated with competition as are the other summary statistics.

The outcomes from testing the null hypotheses in each market for the four summary measures are displayed in Tables 7.2 through 7.5 of analysis of variance results. The numbers in parentheses heading each column are the critical F values for test FP, FL, and FI, at a .05 level of significance. Within the body of each table, entries followed by a double asterisk represent outcomes that exceed the critical F values. Hence, these entries indicate rejection of a null hypothesis of no treatment effect.

In the table of numbers-equivalent results (Table 7.2), policy has a significant impact in 20 markets, law a significant impact in 55 markets, and there is a significant joint effect in 7 markets. Roughly similar results are observed for the other measures as well. In testing the number of banks outcomes, policy significantly influences results in 13 markets, the null hypothesis of no legal impact is rejected in 55 markets, and significant joint effects occur in 5 markets. With the number of branches results, the null hypothesis of no policy effect is rejected in 7 markets, state law has a significant impact in 51 markets, and joint effects are significant in 8 markets. Finally, the concentration ratio is sigfificantly affected by regulatory policy in 21 markets, law is significant in 46 markets, and the interaction between policy and law is significant in 7 markets.

Table 7.2. Numbers-Equivalent

MKT	FP (3.09)	FL (2.70)	FI (2.19)	MKT	FP (3.09)	FL (2.70)	FI (2.19)
1	68.331**	16.951**	2.627**	29	.708	11.547**	.358
2	4.147**	30.609**	.760	30	.411	13.806**	1.237
3	6.147**	33.275**	.989	31	.321	25.682**	1.290
4	6.393**	30.900**	1.808	32	.469	20.370**	1.690
5	17.102**	10.788**	.149	33	2.766	15.537**	.212
6	2.466	30.042**	.711	34	1.538	14.035**	4.53
7	2.056	48.353**	1.462	35	3.738**	11.045**	3.610**
8	5.118**	16.673**	1.585	36	2.204	26.231**	1.230
9	6.096**	20.774**	.301	37	4.848**	20.330**	.212
10	.301	18.618**	.190	38	.262	31.546**	1.958
11	3.929**	54.297**	.427	39	3.519**	14.649**	2.528**
12	.710	14.622**	.664	40	.272	23.938**	2.362**
13	2.573	8.925**	1.335	41	1.375	28.252**	1.134
14	.742	10.681**	1.629	42	.688	11.303**	.112
15	18.629**	23.092**	1.024	43	.515	22.145**	1.238
16	2.260	5.392**	1.705	44	34.119**	21.370**	2.028
17	.200	8.433**	1.012	45	4.118**	17.152**	.041
18	.277	30.954**	1.676	46	35.706**	29.325**	3.721**
19	1.383	24.420**	1.477	47	2.701	10.135**	.643
20	7.844**	12.028**	.546	48	.267	14.679**	2.133
21	1.089	6.790**	.374	49	20.789**	13.332**	1.735
22	.231	3.126**	.938	50	1.070	35.203**	.916
23	2.151	50.063**	2.706**	51	26.055**	5.599**	4.486**
24	.360	18.115**	1.239	52	15.503**	7.980**	.696
25	1.001	9.871**	.347	53	1.771	3.831**	1.079
26	1.361	35.555**	1.479	54	9.769**	23.407**	1.510
27	2.101	58.997**	.647	55	1.057	12.686**	1.887
28	.020	36.220**	1.470				

Table 7.3. Number of Banks

MKT	FP	FL	FI	MKT	FP	FL	FI
	(3.09)	(2.70)	(2.19)		(3.09)	(2.70)	(2.19)
1	13.566**	138.634**	1.238	29	.032	21.428**	.289
2	5.696**	46.430**	.568	30	.519	23.278**	1.687
3	1.476	54.667**	1.190	31	.267	41.561**	1.790
4	2.591	26.012**	.882	32	.025	30.888**	.924
5	14.479**	10.301**	.739	33	2.116	26.165**	1.112
6	1.854	53.308**	1.286	34	1.095	13.039**	.317
7	1.630	80.200**	.927	35	2.450	26.575**	3.108**
8	.668	32.757**	1.751	36	3.022	30.357**	1.322
9	4.340**	21.824**	.341	37	2.124	41.032**	.537
10	.658	35.744**	.184	38	.983	49.389**	2.310**
11	1.420	78.137**	.858	39	1.184	26.421**	1.234
12	.331	7.243**	.542	40	.412	43.160**	1.375
13	.280	27.905**	1.281	41	.380	33.283**	.791
14	3.434**	28.547**	1.932	42	.814	15.295**	.673
15	2.524	47.366**	1.849	43	.533	28.012**	.845
16	2.597	14.067**	3.429**	44	6.825**	66.620**	.925
17	1.195	27.753**	1.970	45	3.215**	25.226**	.700
18	.117	43.066**	2.092	46	6.608**	67.477**	1.157
19	2.231	25.145**	1.519	47	1.422	19.667**	.600
20	8.979**	48.161**	.658	48	.465	27.303**	.879
21	1.351	24.322**	.627	49	4.759**	16.843**	.948
22	.330	15.073**	.838	50	1.979	40.580**	.898
23	1.255	115.454**	1.948**	51	18.865**	25.889**	1.974
24	.869	21.978**	2.267	52	12.403**	68.052**	2.047
25	.962	15.278**	.310	53	1.542	9.295**	.492
26	.017	63.430**	1.840	54	18.243**	51.073**	2.469**
27	2.125	60.545**	1.133	55	.682	14.731**	1.547
28	.279	44.618**	1.180				

Table 7.4. Number of Branches

MKT	FP (3.09)	FL (2.70)	FI (2.19)	MKT	FP (3.09)	FL (2.70)	FI (2.19)
1	1.579	109.369**	.515	29	.721	25.392**	1.878
2	2.790	15.735**	.709	30	.582	16.292**	1.730
3	.021	20.776**	1.183	31	1.109	16.501**	2.269**
4	.448	66.962**	2.304**	32	.543	5.941**	.709
5	9.231**	32.910**	1.256	33	2.246	8.037**	1.394
6	6.734**	17.138**	1.939	34	1.706	11.639**	.808
7	1.105	48.455**	1.088	35	3.622**	19.933**	2.284**
8	3.095**	37.297**	1.247	36	1.681	11.036**	1.278
9	1.133	10.926**	.429	37	1.092	12.632**	1.849
10	.632	23.580**	1.566	38	.022	32.000**	2.751**
11	.124	31.923**	1.676	39	.023	4.257**	.734
12	.207	.450	.432	40	.225	18.098**	2.469**
13	.833	2.048	1.262	41	2.160	28.519**	1.067
14	3.458**	7.598**	1.183	42	1.590	.796	1.341
15	2.748	23.398**	1.171	43	.480	5.847**	1.176
16	.846	7.822**	.438	44	.245	65.329**	1.501
17	.830	8.430**	.547	45	4.964**	8.152**	3.060**
18	.685	15.598**	.902	46	.110	29.995**	1.268
19	2.833	7.741**	.858	47	.826	7.827**	.793
20	2.792	6.971**	.819	48	1.854	5.459**	.968
21	.901	5.973**	1.958	49	2.395	8.240**	1.900
22	2.898	16.165**	2.364**	50	.444	31.517**	1.298
23	1.429	35.172**	1.518	51	1.845	96.436**	.586
24	.546	26.498**	.354	52	1.779	57.214**	.951
25	1.674	6.978**	.876	53	1.225	16.539**	.973
26	.075	33.484**	1.598	54	4.076**	2.513	1.927
27	2.585	43.758**	4.606**	55	.814	12.043**	1.280
28	.527	32.205**	1.595				

Table 7.5. 1.0 – Concentration Ratio

MKT	FP (3.09)	FL (2.70)	FI (2.19)	MKT	FP (3.09)	FL (2.70)	FI (2.19)
1	12.604**	6.190**	3.158**	29	2.125	6.163**	.435
2	4.356**	17.791**	1.666	30	1.112	13.856**	1.709
3	9.518**	9.944**	1.721	31	.610	30.341**	1.360
4	5.729**	19.481**	2.075	32	1.399	11.491**	1.716
5	7.024**	7.482**	.360	33	1.455	1.943	.860
6	2.070	7.451**	.755	34	1.882	7.058**	.807
7	2.930	34.401**	1.390	35	1.364	17.648**	3.391**
8	7.667**	8.166**	1.361	36	.531	25.270**	1.737
9	2.558	9.605**	.426	37	4.979**	5.987**	.130
10	.276	27.093**	.146	38	1.308	41.883**	2.797**
11	2.729	12.574**	.595	39	5.052	6.594**	2.361**
12	.774	32.682**	.912	40	.746	3.735**	1.488
13	6.109**	6.724**	1.302	41	.915	12.808**	.717
14	.174	1.033	.691	42	.691	7.866**	.415
15	9.128**	9.493**	1.932	43	.006	8.117**	1.048
16	1.946	1.141	1.369	44	33.510**	17.436**	1.404
17	.706	4.513**	.736	45	3.582**	8.321**	.173
18	1.384	26.660**	.965	46	63.119**	12.791**	3.236**
19	1.291	8.607**	1.418	47	4.595**	4.498**	.629
20	5.478**	3.305**	.679	48	.716	5.463**	2.041
21	.772	.195	.290	49	25.442**	13.927**	1.863
22	1.687	.325	.770	50	1.234	39.903**	.852
23	8.907**	18.730**	3.943**	51	22.985**	2.605**	5.074**
24	2.512	18.291**	1.043	52	21.106**	2.182**	.625
25	.971	1.574	.579	53	2.791	3.430**	.724
26	4.899**	14.234**	1.666	54	4.969**	8.419**	.647
27	1.815	46.638**	1.236	55	1.774	2.690**	.869
28	.353	30.533**	1.745				

Overall, state law appears to have the most pervasive influence on market structure outcomes. Varying the law affects two to four times as many markets as varying regulatory policy with the market structure measures examined. In addition, the joint impact of law and policy does not appear to have a major influence on the four structural measures. Therefore, market structure outcomes are affected primarily by law and policy working independently. As a final point, regulatory policy is more effective in influencing measures of concentration than measures of service availability. Thus, about twice as many markets are affected by regulatory policy in the numbers-equivalent and concentration ratio measures as in the number of banks and number of branches measures.

The analysis of variance results detailed above merely test for the presence of significant control instrument influence without demonstrating any direction of impact. That is, no test is made to determine whether various instruments are increasing or decreasing measured competition. Thus it is quite possible that certain laws or policies have a significant influence in many local markets by enhancing competition while in other markets they have the opposite impact. In addition, alternative instruments may affect local markets differently.

To investigate whether these effects are actually present, the following illustrative two-step test is constructed.[2] One regulatory policy (actual competition) is specified and held constant. As before, each market and each measure is tested separately.[3] The mean values of a given measure in a given market under alternative laws are first subjected to an F test to determine the existence of significant differences. If a significant difference among the means is present, all paired contrasts (one law's mean result in the market minus a different law's mean result) are tested to identify the source of deviations among means. For example, with the four laws simulated, six t tests of paired contrasts are investigated (statewide versus holding company, statewide versus districtwide, etc.) for each local market whenever the initial F test indicates a significant difference in the market's competitive measure among laws. Since regulatory policy is held constant in these tests, any significant difference between individual means is attributed to a law's influence. All tests are conducted at a .05 significance level.

Tables 7.6 through 7.9 contain summary results of individual market tests. For a given measure, the number of markets displaying a positive contrast (row law mean minus column law mean) is in the upper table, the number of markets yielding a significant negative contrast between laws is in the lower table. (Positive contrasts are associated with enhanced measured competition.) For example, referring to the numbers-equivalent measures in Table 7.6, the statewide law (SW) produces significantly higher numbers-equivalent results in 17 markets when compared to the holding company law (HC) and significantly higher numbers-equivalent measures in 6 markets when contrasted against the districtwide law

Table 7.6. Numbers-Equivalent

Total of Significant Contrasts Greater than 0

	HC	DW	CC
SW	17	6	34
HC		3	8
DW			27

Total of Significant Contrasts Less than 0

	HC	DW	CC
SW	1	0	0
HC		11	0
DW			0

Table 7.7. Number of Banks

Total of Significant Contrasts Greater than 0

	HC	DW	CC
SW	33	13	49
HC		3	8
DW			33

Total of Significant Contrasts Less than 0

	HC	DW	CC
SW	0	0	0
HC		24	0
DW			0

Table 7.8. 3-Bank Concentration Ratio

Total of Significant Contrasts Greater than 0

	HC	DW	CC
SW	9	3	15
HC		4	11
DW			12

Total of Significant Conrasts Less than 0

	HC	DW	CC
SW	4	0	0
HC		7	3
DW			0

Table 7.9. Number of Branches

Total of Significant Contrasts Greater than 0

	HC	DW	CC
SW	8	4	15
HC		9	15
DW			14

Total of Significant Contrasts Less than 0

	HC	DW	CC
SW	9	0	5
HC		8	6
DW			6

(DW). Conversely, the holding company law generates a higher numbers-equivalent than the statewide law in 1 market and the districtwide law does not yield a significantly higher mean numbers-equivalent than the statewide law in any local market.

A similar set of tests is also conducted by holding state law constant (statewide branching) and varying regulatory policy. The summary results from these tests are located in Tables 7.10 through 7.13. These tables read in the same manner as the previous legal results. For example, referring to the numbers-equivalent outcomes (Table 7.10), the potential competition policy (P) produces a significantly greater mean numbers-equivalent than the actual competition policy (A) in 2 markets and a significantly greater mean numbers-equivalent than the historical policy (H) in 3 markets. The lower set of entries in Table 7.10 indicates that the actual competition policy produces a significantly greater mean numbers-equivalent than the potential competition policy in no markets while the historical policy generates a mean result significantly higher than the potential competition policy in 1 market.

Table 7.10. Numbers-Equivalent

Total of Significant Contrasts Greater than 0

	A	H
P	2	3
A		0

Total of Significant Contrasts Less than 0

	A	H
P	0	1
A		0

Table 7.11. Number of Banks

Total of Significant Contrasts Greater than 0

	A	H
P	1	1
A		1

Total of Significant Contrasts Less than 0

	A	H
P	0	1
A		1

Table 7.12. 3-Bank Concentration Ratio

Total of Significant Contrasts Greater than 0

	A	H
P	2	3
A		0

Total of Significant Contrasts Less than 0

	A	H
P	1	0
A		0

Table 7.13. Number of Branches

Total of Significant Contrasts Greater than 0

	A	H
P	0	0
A		1

Total of Significant Contrasts Less than 0

	A	H
P	2	1
A		1

The outcomes of testing the various paired contrasts across laws and across policies suggest two main conclusions. First, more liberal laws like statewide branching appear to engender increased local market competition when compared to more restrictive laws like contiguous county expansion. At the same time, regulatory policy alone seems to have little if any impact given the particular law (statewide branching) specified for the analysis. Second, the competitive impact of particular instruments is not uniform. Since a given law or policy does not affect all local markets in the same fashion, no control instrument has an unambiguous influence. Thus, given this demonstrated differential impact of laws and policies across local markets, it is clearly important to choose structural control instruments with reference to some unified weighting, aggregation, and valuation scheme.

The statistical tests conducted on the simulation results should be viewed with some caution. The simulation outcomes obtained for the structural measures are not independent under various laws and policies because many common factors influence all the results. For example, in each policy-legal combination, the same initial conditions are specified and bank behavior remains invariate. In addition, the general operation and flow process of the simulation may generate complex and nonobvious biases that influence all outcomes similarly. Thus, although the null hypotheses cannot be perfectly tested, the significance tests give some indication of the relative strengths and joint effects of the instruments. Moreover, while it appears clear that state law is a more potent structural control instrument than regulatory policy, this statistical analysis says little about how preferred instruments might be chosen. In Chapter VIII, a comprehensive procedure for selecting banking structure control instruments is developed.

NOTES

1. This discussion of analysis of variance is taken from Freund [15] pp. 342-345.

2. The procedure is known as Scheffe's method of multiple post hoc comparisons. It is used because it can be employed with different numbers of observations and because it is not overly sensitive to nonnormality and unequal variances.

3. As before, all three-bank concentration ratio results reported below are transformed to 1–CR3.

APPENDIX

This appendix compares the results of one 1971 simulation iteration with the actual mergers and de novo branches that occurred in 1971. A direct comparison is difficult because the simulation operates through stochastic processes and the outcomes of any one iteration may diverge widely from mean results. However, the results presented here are illustrative of the simulation's operation.

The tables are read in the following fashion. The columns on the left side give actual outcomes for 1971. The first row shows that bank 034, a class 1 initiator headquartered in market 46 (see map in Chapter V) actually merged with bank number 901, a class 5 bank, which was headquartered in market 46. The columns on the right give simulation outcomes for 1971. In the third row, the simulation also combines bank 034 and bank 901. The de novo branch tables are read in a similar fashion.

Table 7.14. Merger Simulation.

Actual 1971 Acquisitions						Simulation of 1971 Acquisitions					
Bank number	Initiator class	Home market	Bank number	Partner class	Home market	Bank number	Initiator class	Market number	Bank number	Partner class	Home market
034	1	46	901	5	46	031	1	46	020	5	46
088	1	4	516	5	5	031	1	46	028	4	46
698	1	1	220	4	3	034	1	46	901	5	46
						611	1	1	134	3	1
						622	1	1	692	3	1
						697	1	1	694	4	1
						697	1	1	691	4	1
284	2	49	919	5	49	303	2	15	730	5	20
452	2	9	908	4	7	354	2	44	390	5	54
536	2	8	600	4	7	536	2	8	526	5	8
643	2	5	903	5	5						
643	2	5	185	5	5						
554	3	24	115	5	25						
263	4	28	207	4	29	151	4	42	158	5	42
414	4	41	913	5	46	152	4	42	767	4	42
453	4	9	906	5	9	160	4	42	764	5	42
800	4	26	912	5	27	203	4	29	256	5	29
801	4	26	116	4	25	311	4	19	742	5	20
310	5	19	660	5	19	811	5	23	594	5	30

Table 7.15. De Novo Branch Simulation

Actual 1971 De Novo Branches				Simulation of 1971 De Novo Branches			
Bank number	Class	Home market	Market chosen	Bank number	Class	Home market	Market chosen
029	1	46	46	029	1	46	46
031	1	46	46	029	1	46	46
031	1	46	46	029	1	46	46
034	1	46	46	029	1	46	46
088	1	4	4	029	1	46	46
088	1	4	1	031	1	46	39
468	1	13	4	031	1	46	46
612	1	1	1	033	1	46	39
612	1	1	1	033	1	46	46
612	1	1	1	034	1	46	45
612	1	1	1	034	1	46	39
613	1	1	1	034	1	46	46
613	1	1	1	034	1	46	53
613	1	1	1	034	1	46	46
619	1	1	1	611	1	1	1
619	1	1	3	611	1	1	3
621	1	1	1	611	1	1	1
621	1	1	1	612	1	1	1
622	1	1	1	612	1	1	1
622	1	1	1	613	1	1	1
622	1	1	1	613	1	1	1
622	1	1	1	613	1	1	1
622	1	1	1	619	1	1	2
622	1	1	1	619	1	1	5
697	1	1	1	619	1	1	1
697	1	1	1	621	1	1	1
697	1	1	1	621	1	1	3
697	1	1	1	622	1	1	5
697	1	1	1	697	1	1	5
697	1	1	1	697	1	1	1
698	1	1	1	698	1	1	5
089	2	4	4	101	2	34	33
283	2	52	51	284	2	49	51
283	2	52	51	304	2	15	5
303	2	15	15	304	2	15	4
320	2	1	1	362	2	32	15
342	2	51	51				
342	2	51	51				
354	2	44	44				
510	2	5	5				
511	2	5	5				
536	2	8	8				
643	2	5	5				
821	2	49	48				

Actual bk.no.	Class	Ho.mkt.	Mkt.chosen	Simulation bk.no.	Class	Ho.mkt.	Mkt.chosen
822	2	49	49				
830	2	38	38				
134	3	1	1	154	3	42	46
134	3	1	5	154	3	42	29
292	3	15	15	154	3	42	46
415	3	41	40	415	3	41	40
482	3	53	53	580	3	52	49
482	3	53	53	582	3	52	52
554	3	24	26	601	3	7	5
866	3	46	46	601	3	7	5
				624	3	1	1
				644	3	5	1
				840	3	54	54
				840	3	54	54
008	4	17	17	007	4	17	32
008	4	17	17	043	4	46	46
023	4	46	46	046	4	47	47
024	4	46	46	071	4	33	42
103	4	34	34	117	4	25	9
116	4	25	26	141	4	48	48
116	4	25	25	224	4	2	1
116	4	25	26	251	4	35	42
152	4	42	42	270	4	22	5
203	4	29	29	273	4	22	5
263	4	28	28	422	4	40	40
263	4	28	28	454	4	9	8
270	4	22	22	474	4	13	19
311	4	19	19	494	4	14	4
369	4	32	32	537	4	8	25
401	4	31	31	570	4	37	49
414	4	41	40	667	4	21	25
440	4	9	9	735	4	20	21
456	4	9	9	760	4	43	46
462	4	13	13	800	4	26	24
593	4	30	30	865	4	45	46
623	4	1	1	865	4	45	46
694	4	1	1	892	4	16	16
739	4	20	20	894	4	17	13
002	5	17	17	003	5	17	17
402	5	31	31	072	5	33	33
492	5	14	14	185	5	5	5
551	5	24	24	223	5	3	2
640	5	5	5	241	5	39	39

Actual bk.no.	Class	Ho.mkt.	Mkt.chosen	Simulation bk.no.	Class	Ho.mkt.	Mkt.chosen
651	5	5	5	252	5	34	35
683	5	18	18	261	5	28	28
764	5	42	42	525	5	8	5
791	5	10	10	556	5	24	24
850	5	11	12	654	5	5	1
				853	5	11	11
				881	5	25	25
				882	5	9	9
				882	5	9	9

Chapter VIII

An Analytic Framework
for Policy Decision

The simulation results generate quantitative measures of local market structure for each of the state's local banking markets. The prior chapter detailed statistical methods for comparing the projected summary measures under different regulatory policy and state law combinations. It was shown that the alternative policies and laws create statistically significant differences in final period local market structures. However, policy choice is difficult without a unified framework to evaluate projected outcomes. This chapter suggests a cohesive analytic structure for regulatory and legal decisions.

THE GENERAL CONTEXT OF
BANKING STRUCTURE CONTROL

The basic assumption underlying the control of merging, branching, and holding company expansion in the commercial banking industry links regulation of banks' organizational and market structures to the generation of a socially desirable combination of safety, availability, and competition in the production of banking services. However, these objectives are not always mutually reinforcing. A large number of banking alternatives are generally understood to foster competitive pricing, but unrestrained competition is sometimes viewed as a threat to service availability and safety. Moreover, no consensus concerning an optimal banking structure has been reached by the various state and federal regulatory agencies. Instead, a large number of alternative legal and regulatory rules have evolved in efforts to promote public welfare. The objective of the following analysis is to detail methods for selecting preferred banking structure control procedures.

The choice of a unique regulatory policy and state law combination is particularly difficult due to four institutional factors. First, any regulatory-legal combination must apply uniformly to all local banking markets and individual expansion attempts. Second, incomplete control over market structure is exercised under most feasible alternatives.[1] Competitive outcomes are generally the result of interaction between bank initiated expansions and exogenous policy control procedures rather than simple regulatory or legal fiat. Third, control procedures have a dynamic impact on structure through time. Since this multiperiod impact is not well understood or predictable, various imperfect measures such as bank size, location, and market share are used as proxy measures to weigh the likely long run influence of individual decisions. Fourth, structural control instruments are not subject to frequent change. It is both politically and legally difficult to frequently alter regulatory policy or state law. Because of these four factors, it is important to understand the long-run implications of any regulatory policy or law under consideration.

A METHOD FOR EVALUATING
PROJECTED MARKET STRUCTURE

A direct method for evaluating alternative regulatory policies and state laws is to assume that the various agencies concerned with influencing a state's banking structure share a common utility function.[2] Let this utility function have as arguments horizon period competition (C), safety (S), and availability (A) in banking service provision.

$$(1) \qquad V_R = V(C,S,A); \frac{\partial V_R}{\partial C} > 0, \quad \frac{\partial V_R}{\partial S} > 0, \quad \frac{\partial V_R}{\partial A} > 0.$$

Two basic problems in the analysis of market structure are immediately evident. First, C, S, and A cannot be directly measured. Instead, various proxy variables such as number of banks, number of offices, or a concentration measure must be employed to gauge structural outcomes. It is assumed that C, S, and A are functionally related to these proxy variables. A second difficulty concerns control instrument impact on local banking markets. Regulatory policies and state laws must apply uniformly to all local banking markets. However, while policies and laws are defined on a statewide basis, the performance of control instruments is evaluated on the basis of local market results. Hence, some method for aggregating local market outcomes must be developed.

One method for surmounting these difficulties entails defining a statewide aggregate index of local market structure. As an example of this procedure, let the index be a function of the proxy measures that structural control instruments partially determine:

$$(2) \qquad \psi = \psi(M_1, M_2, \ldots, M_j).$$

A simple ψ is defined as a linear combination of three aggregate measures:

$$(3) \qquad \psi = a_1 M_1 + a_2 M_2 + a_3 M_3.$$

> M_1: Composite numbers-equivalent;
> M_2: Composite number of banks;
> M_3: Composite number of offices.

An M_j is the aggregate of each local market's structure measure weighted by market population.

The number of banks (M_2) and number of offices (M_3) variables capture aspects of structure not adequately measured by the aggregate number's equivalent (M_1). A large number of banks and offices, even in a highly concentrated market, gives some indication of the convenience dimension of structural control. In addition, bank safety is reflected to some degree by the number of banks per unit population operating in a market. That is, for a market with a given population, an extremely large number of banks that compete vigorously may be viewed as excessively competitive and unstable. To the extent that regulatory agencies are concerned with bank failures, the security of existing banks can be measured by the number of banks and degree of competition in local markets.

Each of the arguments (C, S, and A) of the utility function may be defined as functions of ψ:

(4) $\quad C = C(\psi),\ C > 0,$

(5) $\quad S = S(\psi),\ S > 0,$

(6) $\quad A = A(\psi),\ A > 0.$

By substituting for C, S, and A, the utility function can be expresssed as a function of ψ:

(7) $\quad V_R = V[C(\psi),\ S(\psi),\ A(\psi)];$

(8) $\quad V_R = Z(\psi);\ V'_R \gtreqless 0,\ V''_R < 0.$

The utility function (8) is not a monotonic function of ψ because safety considerations eventually outweigh the desirability of additional competition or service availability. Thus the functional relationship between V_R and ψ is concave from below.

A composite structure measure can be constructed in the following fashion. The M_j are composed of each ith local market's structure value m_{ji}, weighted by the market's population P_i. Aggregation is multiplicative:

(9) $\quad M_j = [\prod_{i=1}^{55} \frac{(m_{ji})}{P_i}]^{1/55}$

Thus M_j is the geometric mean of local market m_{ji} per unit population.

Composite measures of market structure aggregated in the indicated fashion have several advantageous properties. Deflating each market's competitive measure by local market population yields a weighted indicator of actual banking performance. A market with a small population cannot support the number of banks or banking offices that can flourish in a heavily populated market. In addition, aggregation through the geometric mean mechanism directly incorporates distributional aspects of structure across markets. That is, the overbanked and underbanked markets do not net out in aggregation as may occur with a linear aggregation scheme. Since the simulated impact of alternative control instrument combinations occurs through their influence on the distribution of banking facilities among local markets, it is essential that the statewide index measure this aspect of structure across local banking markets. A concrete example illustrates the point. Let

$$(10) \quad M = [\prod_{h=1}^{n} \frac{(m_h)}{P_h}]^{1/n}$$

represent a structure measure. For simplicity, suppose only a single measure M is employed. The objective is to evaluate the conditions for utility maximization with respect to the local market measures of M.

$$(11) \quad \text{Max } V_R = Z(\psi(M))$$
$$\{m_h\};$$

$$(12) \quad \frac{\partial V_R}{m_i} = \frac{\partial V_R}{\partial \psi} \cdot \frac{\partial \psi}{\partial M} \cdot \left(\frac{M^{-1}}{nP_i}\left[\prod_{h \neq i}^{n}\left(\frac{m_h}{P_h}\right)\right]\right) = 0 ;$$

$$(13) \quad \frac{\partial V_R}{\partial m_k} = \frac{\partial V_R}{\partial \psi} \cdot \frac{\partial \psi}{\partial M} \cdot \left(\frac{M^{-1}}{nP_R}\left[\prod_{h \neq R}^{n}\left(\frac{m_h}{P_h}\right)\right]\right) = 0 .$$

Utility maximization implies that the ratio of marginal utilities $\left(\frac{\partial V_R}{\partial m_i} / \frac{\partial V_R}{\partial m_k}\right)$ equals the ratio of weights $(1/P_i, 1/P_k)$ assigned to markets i and k. Forming the ratio and cancelling common terms gives

$$(14) \quad \frac{m_k/P_iP_k}{m_k/P_iP_k} = \frac{1/P_i}{1/P_k} .$$

Rearranging this expression yields a simple equality between market i and market k ratios for utility maximization (asterisks denote optimal values):

(15) $$\left(\frac{m_k}{P_k}\right)^* = \left(\frac{m_i}{P_i}\right)^*.$$

Equation (15) indicates that aggregate market structure yields maximum utility when there is zero variance among population weighted local market measures. This is an extremely desirable property for an index concerned with measuring the statewide impact of instruments that must apply uniformly to all local markets.

Given the statewide aggregate structure index ψ, a particular single period utility function can be defined. As outlined in the initial discussion of the structural control agencies' utility function, the control objectives of competition, safety, and service availability imply a utility function that is concave from below with respect to ψ. An expression quadratic in ψ yields a simple functional form that satisfies the concavity properties specified for V_R. Thus define

(16) $$V_R = \beta_1\psi - \beta_2\psi^2.$$

Since the outcomes of control influence are uncertain, the regulatory-legal objective is to identify a structure that maximizes the expected value of V_R:

(17) $$E(V_R) = \beta_1 E(\psi) - \beta_2 [E(\psi)]^2 - \beta_2 \sigma^2(\psi);$$

where

(18) $$E(\psi) = a_1 E(M_1) + a_2 E(M_2) + a_3 E(M_3);$$

(19) $$\sigma^2(\psi) = A^2\sigma_{M_1}^2 = a_2^2\sigma_{M_2}^2 + a_3^2\sigma_{M_3}^2 + 2a_1 a_2 \text{cov}(M_1, M_2)$$
$$+ 2a_1 a_3 \text{cov}(M_1, M_3) + 2a_2 a_3 \text{cov}(M_2, M_3).$$

Note that all expected values and variances are computed across simulation iterations, not across markets. That is, each M_i is aggregated for the given simulation iteration. Then the expected values and variances are computed across iterations' aggregate M_i.

If a set of policies existed that allowed continuous variation of aggregate structure measures, a policy could be adopted to exactly achieve an unconstrained optimal banking structure. In reality, only a discrete number of regulatory policy-state law combinations are available. This group of feasible structural control alternatives defines a constraint set that limits unrestricted expected utility maximization. Hence, within the analytic framework described above, the problem facing the structural control agencies is to maximize $E(V_R)$ subject to the constraint set of available policies. This is an integer programming problem since a finite and discrete instrument must be selected. However, when a fairly small number of feasible alternatives exists, $E(V_R)$ can be directly computed for each alternative and a best feasible regulatory-legal combination chosen. The simulation output, which gives $E(\psi)$ and $\sigma^2(\psi)$ for a specific set of twelve feasible alternatives, allows such choice.

AN ILLUSTRATION OF CONTROL PROCEDURE EVALUATION

Evaluation of the simulation's terminal period market structure projections proceeds with the functional forms for V_R and ψ previously detailed once weights for the aggregate structure index and parameters for the utility function are specified. The weights and parameters employed in this section are completely arbitrary. However, they allow the development of a precise example of policy-legal choice in banking structure control that illustrates how the evaluation process might work. In addition, a sensitivity analysis with different index weights demonstrates the strengths and weaknesses of the analytic framework.

To initiate the analysis, certain a priori conditions must be specified for the m_{ji}/P_i that comprise the M_j. First, suppose an optimal arrangement for a local market implies that all banks are equal in size. This means the numbers-equivalent equals the number of banks and concentration is minimized given the number of banks operating in the market. Second, for safety considerations, let 3000 people per bank and 1000 people per office be the local banking intensity that the control agencies perceive optimal on the bases of competition, availability, and safety. These conditions imply (with population expressed in thousands)

$$(20a) \qquad \left(\frac{m_{1i}}{P_i}\right)^* = \left(\frac{m_{2i}}{P_i}\right)^*;$$

(20b) $$\left(\frac{m_{2i}}{P_i}\right)^* = \frac{1}{3} \; ;$$

(20c) $$\left(\frac{m_{3i}}{P_i}\right)^* = 1.$$

The M_j aggregation rule (9) means that $M_j = m_{ji}/P_i$ if $m_{ji}/P_i = m_{jk}/P_k$ for   i, k local markets. Thus the optimal values for the aggregate M_j are

(21a) $$M_1^* = \frac{1}{3} \; ;$$

(21b) $$M_2^* = \frac{1}{3} \; ;$$

(21c) $$M_3^* = 1 \; ;$$

(21d) with $\sigma(M_i, M_j) = 0$ for all i, j.

In addition, let the following weights be assigned to the M_j comprising ψ, where ψ is defined as a linear combination of the M_j:

(22) $$\psi = a_1 M_1 + a_2 M_2 + a_3 M_3;$$

and

$$a_1 = 100;$$
$$a_2 = 75;$$
$$a_3 = 30.$$

This set of weights emphasizes competition rather than service availability in ψ. Hence the weight assigned to the aggregate numbers-equivalent (a_1) is more than three times greater than the weight associated with the aggregate number of offices (a_3). The aggregate number of banks (a_2) is also heavily weighted. The size of (a_2) indicates that the presence of multiple banking organizations is perceived to have a substantial effect on competition that is not entirely captured in the numbers-equivalent measure.

Reference to some specific markets illustrates the weights' influence (see Table 8.1). If all local markets evolve to a structure identical (population weighted) to the projected 1982 Philadelphia market, ψ would equal about seven with the statewide law and the actual competition regulatory policy.[3] Alternatively, if all markets resemble the projected 1982 Bedford market, ψ would equal about seventy under the same regulatory-legal regime.[4]

Table 8.1. Mean Outcomes for Selected Markets
with an Actual Competition Regulatory Policy

Selected Markets (Population in thousands)	1971 Starting Statistics	CC	1982 Two- District	HC	SW
Philadelphia (3635.8):					
Numbers-equivalent	9.5	8.8	9.1	8.6	9.2
Number of banks	27	29	42	32	48
Number of offices	521	776	714	665	697
Pittsburgh (2202.7):					
Numbers-equivalent	5.3	5.0	5.4	5.6	5.6
Number of banks	39	38	45	53	57
Number of offices	345	492	472	443	473
Harrisburg (242.1):					
Numbers-equivalent	7.0	7.2	7.7	8.9	7.8
Number of banks	14	18	21	27	23
Number of offices	54	75	74	94	74
Reading (379.3):					
Numbers-equivalent	7.5	8.6	8.9	11.2	9.4
Number of banks	17	30	33	40	37
Number of offices	67	114	100	133	101
Bedford (43.4):					
Number-equivalent	6.8	9.1	10.8	8.4	11.5
Number of banks	8	12	15	11	16
Number of offices	13	21	25	26	26
Millersburg-Lykens (38.1):					
Numbers-equivalent	8.7	15.0	18.2	14.1	18.3
Number of banks	10	19	23	19	23
Number of offices	15	30	34	35	33

An optimal measure for ψ is obtained directly from the M^*_j calculated previously and the weights assigned to these measures:

(23) $$\psi^* = a_1 M^*_1 + a_2 M^*_2 + a_3 M^*_3,$$

(24) $$\psi^* = 100(1/3) + 75(1/3) + 30(1) = 88.33.$$

Since ψ^* represents an optimal value for ψ, expression (24) combined with the utility function yields relative values for the parameters β_1 and β_2:

(25) $$V_R = \beta_1 \psi - \beta_2 \psi^2.$$

Maximizing V_R with respect to ψ gives an expression for ψ^* in terms of β_1 and β_2:

(26) $$\frac{\partial V_R}{\partial^! V} = \beta_1 - 2\beta_2\psi = 0;$$

(27) $$\psi^* = \frac{\beta_1}{2\beta_2}.$$

Expressions (24) and (27) mean

(28) $$\frac{\beta_1}{2\beta_2} = 88.33.$$

Define $\beta_1 = 100$;
then $\beta_2 = 0.57$.

These parameters allow a precise specification of the expected utility function:

(29) $$E(V_R) = 100E(\psi) - 0.57[E(\psi)]^2 - 0.57\sigma^2(\psi).$$

In a coordinate system with $E(\psi)$ and $\sigma(\psi)$ axes, the expected utility function generates semicircular indifference curves centered on $E(\psi) = 88.33$ and $\sigma(\psi) = 0$.

The projected outcome for each of the simulation's regulatory-legal combinations can be depicted in the same $\{E(\psi), \sigma(\psi)\}$ space. Table 8.2 details the relevant values for each alternative.

Table 8.2.

Case	Policies	$E(\psi)$	$\sigma\psi$	$E(V_R)$
A1	SW-P	37.36	0.68	2945.55
A2	SW-A	37.44	1.05	2949.02
A3	SW-H	36.52	1.18	2896.16
A4	HC-P	31.36	0.61	2575.22
A5	HC-A	31.90	0.47	2609.83
A6	HC-H	31.73	0.72	2598.83
A7	DW-P	34.98	1.12	2799.83
A8	DW-A	34.71	0.75	2783.83
A9	DW-H	34.62	0.81	2781.48
A10	CC-P	29.32	0.75	2441.67
A11	CC-A	28.90	0.66	2413.68
A12	CC-H	28.45	0.65	2383.40

Figure 8.1 gives a graphical representation of the regulatory-legal alternatives in the $\{E(\psi), \sigma(\psi)\}$ coordinate system. (Note that the

scale-changes on both axes make the semicircular indifference curves appear almost linear.) The $E(V_R)$ values given in Table 8.2 and depicted in Figure 8.1 show that alternative A2 is the preferred regulatory-legal combination. Thus on the basis of this horizon period analysis, the structural control agencies would prefer an actual competition regulatory policy and a statewide branching law.

Several additional conclusions can be drawn from this analysis of simulation outcomes. First, the $E(\psi), \sigma(\psi)$ outcomes are generally clustered for each state law. Thus state law is a more powerful structural control instrument than regulatory policy among the alternatives tested. However, this conclusion may not be true if more extreme regulatory policy is dominant for each state law. For example, from Table 8.2, the actual competition rule works best for the statewide and holding company laws but the potential competition policy works best for the districtwide and contiguous county laws. This means that it may not be desirable to formulate a single federal regulatory policy for application to all states' banking industries.

It is possible that the ranking of alternatives depicted in Table 8.2 depends upon the weights (a_j) used to construct ψ. To

FIGURE 8.1

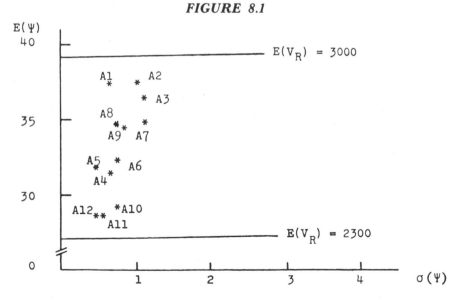

investigate how the a_j influence ψ, a sensitivity analysis employing two polar cases is utilized. The initial trial developed above is labeled case I. As noted before, the ψ in case I contains a balance of all three structural dimensions. In case II, the total focus in ψ is directed toward concentration. This is achieved by specifying the following weights for the M_j:

$a_1 = 265;$
$a_2 = 0;$
$a_3 = 0.$

This weighting scheme also maintains the parameters of $E(V_R)$. **Case III reflects a total interest in the number of banking organizations. Neither concentration nor service availability directly enter** ψ.[5] Without altering the form of $E(V_R)$, this ψ is obtained by setting:

$a_1 = 0;$
$a_2 = 265;$
$a_3 = 0.$

Table 8.3 gives the $E(V_R)$ values and regulatory-legal ranking for all three trials.

Table 8.3.

	Case I ($a_1 = 100$; $a_2 = 75$; $a_3 = 30$)	Case II ($a_1 = 265$; $a_2 = 0$; $a_3 = 0$)	Case III ($a_1 = 0$; $a_2 = 265$; $a_3 = 0$)
	Alternative $E(V_R)$	Alternative $E(V_R)$	Alternative $E(V_R)$
1)	SW-A: 2949.02	SW-A: 2250.04	SW-P: 3664.49
2)	SW-P: 2945.55	SW-P: 2239.02	SW-A: 3663.84
3)	SW-H: 2896.16	SW-H: 2184.43	SW-H: 3618.64
4)	DW-P: 2799.83	DW-P: 2143.48	DW-P: 3452.52
5)	DW-A: 2783.83	DW-A: 2132.15	DW-A: 3404.52
6)	DW-H: 2781.48	DW-H: 2094.39	DW-H: 3399.94
7)	HC-A: 2609.83	HC-A: 2001.46	HC-A: 3066.78
8)	HC-H: 2598.83	HC-H: 1977.87	HC-H: 3057.15
9)	HC-P: 2575.22	HC-P: 1965.71	HC-P: 3023.61
10)	CC-P: 2441.67	CC-P: 1851.88	CC-P: 2877.18
11)	CC-A: 2413.68	CC-A: 1820.02	CC-A: 2837.22
12)	CC-H: 2383.40	CC-H: 1771.13	CC-H: 2804.10

Three major items of interest are apparent in Table 8.3. First, only one regulatory-legal pair changes rank across the three weighting systems. This is the switch in position in case III between SW-P and SW-A. Thus SW-A is the second ranking combination of instruments only in case III. However, even in case III, SW-A places a very close second to SW-P. Hence the ranking of regulatory-legal options does not appear to be very sensitive to different a_j. Second, the expected utility values generated by different weighting schemes are not identical. This reflects variable performance among the M_j. A primary factor concerns the relationship between M_1 and M_2. It is more difficult to approach an optimal numbers-equivalent than an optimal number of banks because any size bank operating in a market counts equally in M_2 but not in M_1. Another factor concerns M_3. Because of extensive branching under all alternatives, near optimal (m_{3i}/P_i) values in many markets are not uncommon. Both these details explain why case I expected utility values surpass case II results. The first factor accounts for the case III expected utility values exceeding either case I or case II. A final interesting observation in Table 8.3 pertains to the least desirable regulatory-legal combination. In each case, the lowest ranking alternative is a continuation of the present state law with the historical regulatory policy.

In summary, this analysis of simulation results illustrates several important aspects of banking structure control. On the one hand, it is evident that influencing banking structure evolution through control instruments is an extremely complex procedure. A suboptimal combination of state law and federal regulatory policy may be implemented if the control agencies do not have a well-considered framework for defining and enforcing instruments to channel market structure outcomes. On the other hand, the example developed above shows one possible scheme for aggregating, weighting, and ranking projected outcomes. This example demonstrates the feasibility of using a simulation model with a comprehensive analytic framework to investigate the cumulative impact of various control instruments.

NOTES

1. A unit banking law with no holding companies precludes structural change through external expansion.

2. See Ali and Greenbaum [1] and Horowitz [24] for earlier discussions of this type of analysis.

3. $\psi = 100 \left(\dfrac{9.2}{3635.8}\right) + 75\left(\dfrac{48}{3635.8}\right) + 30\left(\dfrac{697}{3635.8}\right) = 7.$

4. All population figures are 1970 census data.

5. A third extreme case, total concentration on the number of banking offices, is not developed because no branching regulatory policy is included in the model.

Chapter IX

Summary and Conclusions

Commercial banking in the United States is subject to extensive regulatory and legal constraint. One important feature of this supervision concerns the application of control instruments at both the state and federal levels to influence the evolution of banking market structure. Up to the present time, the implementation of instruments designed to channel bank expansion has been largely ad hoc. The eventual competitive consequences of state laws that define specific and inflexible expansion constraints and federal regulatory policies that proceed on a case by case basis have been largely unknown.

Considerable research has been conducted on issues related to the control of banking market structure. Detailed econometric analysis of bank operating costs has sought to identify economies of scale in the operations of commercial banks and branching networks. No substantial economies are found for banks greater than some minimal size and significant branching diseconomies are manifest.[1] Thus, cost incentives for multioffice operations do not appear sufficient to explain external expansion behavior. However, studies of bank branching behavior based upon statistical analyses of observed choices indicate that expansion decisions can be

121

modeled.[2] In addition, while two more general analyses[3] investigate the evolution of a state's banking industry as a whole, no existing study fits together the disparate evidence to form a cohesive tool for testing the impact of laws and policies on the competitive structures in local banking markets.

Using a unified model of external expansion, this study is focused toward three major problems in banking structure control. First, a comprehensive and versatile experimental methodology is constructed to investigate and test the influences of a wide variety of structural control instruments. The simulation model allows experimentation with several banking laws and regulatory policies although the influences of these instruments are complex and cannot be explicitly detailed. Through the simulation technique, the cumulative market outcomes that result from particular regulatory-legal combinations can be measured. The second and third issues addressed in the study are theoretical. It is demonstrated that alternative laws and policies, including nonextreme variations of existing instruments, have a significant structural impact in local banking markets during the course of the simulated time period. Thus, while Yeats' study[4] illuminates the effect of extremely restrictive policies on a statewide basis, the present study shows that even fairly weak changes in current law and policy can generate measurable local market results. In addition, a general analytic framework for control instrument choice is developed. While the problems in banking structure control are extremely complicated, a coherent regulatory-legal choice procedure is readily applicable. Coupling this decision framework with the simulation methodology allows identification of preferred legal and regulatory alternatives.

The specification of operating rules for this study's simulation model illustrates several interesting procedures for the investigation of issues in banking structural control. First, the various provisions of state banking laws can be defined as operational constraints that limit bank expansion activity. That is, a given law can be represented by rules that constrain the organizational and geographical choice sets of initiating banks. In addition, historical regulatory decisions can be used to estimate a statistical representation of past federal regulatory policy. Moreover, the procedures utilized to estimate the historical policy (i.e., discriminant analysis based upon each proposal's characteristics) suggest techniques for specifying hypothetical regulatory policies. Rather than requiring a detailed explanation of decisions on each constructed example, only an accept or reject response must be elicited for each hypothetical case. Further, soliciting opinions from several experts on bank regulation also reduces individual idiosyncracies in case evaluation. Finally, in the behavioral section of the model, the equations that control the simulation's bank expansion activity give valuable insight into the merger partner choice and de novo market selection processes. The appropriate screening and transformation technique developed allows an accurate and unbiased reconstruction of actual choice situations. This suggests that, while the estimation procedures are used here only to provide the necessary behavioral equations for the simulation, these techniques also can be used to investigate related banking structure issues.

The experiments conducted in the present simulation study with twelve combinations of state laws and federal regulatory policies suggest four general conclusions. First, among the combinations tested, both legal and regulatory treatments can have a significant impact on measured competition in local banking markets. By constraining individual bank's expansion choice sets, these control instruments have a pervasive influence on the competitive structure of a state's banking industry. Moreover, this result is obtained in the absence of any extremely restrictive instrument such as a unit banking law or a no merger regulatory policy. Second, law and regulatory policy appear to operate independently in most local banking markets. That is, law and policy do not interact to magnify or dampen each other's separate effect. This is especially important because it implies that a policy and law that appear desirable separately do not combine to form an undesirable matching of instruments. Third, regulatory policy appears to influence concentration measures more than convenience measures while law has the opposite effect. Thus, law and policy can complement each other in influencing composite structure. The final result bears on the relative impacts of legal and regulatory instruments. Among the alternative state laws and federal regulatory policies tested, state law appears much more powerful than regulatory policy in influencing the competitive outcomes in local banking markets. Hence, state legislatures apparently exercise the dominant structural control.

Given the projections generated by the simulation, some scheme must be constructed to evaluate the structural implications of different laws and policies. Many of the measured differences in local market results created by alternative policy and legal treatments are quite small. For example, a difference between 20 and 22 banks operating in a market may be statistically significant but of little apparent consequence. To gauge the "importance" of such results, a unified aggregation and valuation scheme is developed. The aggregation rule generates statewide structural measures based on simulated local market results. Although different laws and policies may cause only slight divergences in results in each market, when the outcomes are summarized on a statewide basis substantial differences among alternative instruments can be created. Moreover, a distributional property inherent in the aggregation rule implies that instruments with an even impact across local markets tend to display a better measured performance than instruments that have a variable impact across markets. This property is desirable where laws and policies must be formulated for the state as a whole.

Once an aggregate structure index is developed, the measure can be used as a target variable for structural control agencies. The objectives of structural control are assumed to consist primarily of promoting competition, safety, and service availability in a state's banking system. In addition, it is assumed that the structural control agencies can pursue these objectives by using regulatory and legal instruments to influence the value of the aggregate structure variable. The uncertain and dynamic impacts of these instruments are incorporated in the decision rules and monte carlo processes in the simulation. As a result, by analyzing the frequency distributions of outcomes generated by the model, preferred instruments can be identified with an expected utility maximization procedure. In addition, the construction of a reasonable example—

coupled with a sensitivity analysis of the arbitrary parameters in the example—demonstrates that the suggested choice procedure creates implications consistent with the statistical analysis of simulated local market results. That is, state law more powerfully influences structural outcomes than federal regulatory policy and the impacts of the legal and regulatory instruments are largely independent. Finally, given the arbitrary nature of the example, a pairing of the statewide law with the actual competition regulatory policy appears to generate superior measured results.

NOTES

1. See Bell and Murphy [3] and Mullineaux [34] for particularly rigorous studies.
2. Gilbert [18].
3. Yeats [45] and Junker and Oldfield [28].
4. Yeats [45].

References

[1] Ali, Mukhtar M., and Stuart I. Greenbaum. "The Regulatory Process in Commercial Banking," in *Proceedings of a Conference on Bank Structure and Competition*. Federal Reserve Bank of Chicago, 1972.

[2] Austin, Douglas V. "Guidelines for Assessing Potential Competition," in *Proceedings of a Conference on Bank Structure and Competition*. Federal Reserve Bank of Chicago, 1970.

[3] Bell, Frederick W., and Neil B. Murphy. *Costs in Commercial Banking: A Quantitative Analysis of Bank Behavior and Its Relation to Bank Regulation*. Federal Reserve Bank of Boston, 1968.

[4] Brainard, William. "Uncertainty and the Effectiveness of Policy," *American Economic Review* 57 (1967): 411–25.

[5] Carter, Eugene E., and Kalman J. Cohen. "The Use of Simulation in Selecting Branch Banks," *Industrial Management Review* 8 (1967): 55–69.

[6] Cohen, Kalman J., and Frederick S. Hammer. *Analytical Methods in Banking*. Homewood, Ill.: Richard D. Irwin, 1966.

[7] Cohen, Kalman J., and Samuel R. Reid. "Effect of Regulation, Branching and Mergers on Banking Structure and Performance," *Southern Economic Journal* 34 (1967): 231–49.

[8] Cohen, Kalman J., and Samuel R. Reid. "Benefits and Costs of Bank Mergers," *Journal of Financial and Quantitative Analysis* 1 (1966): 15–57.

[9] Cooley, William W., and Paul R. Lohnes. *Multivariate Procedures for the Behavioral Sciences*. New York: John Wiley and Sons, 1962.

[10] Crosse, Howard D. "Banking Structure and Competition," *Journal of Finance* 20 (1965): 349–57.

[11] Davidson, Frederick. "Demand Forecasting for Branch Bank Location Analysis," (Unpublished Ph.D. Thesis): University of Pittsburgh, 1968.

127

[12] Eisenbeis, Robert A., and Robert B. Avery. *Discriminant Analysis and Classification Procedures: Theory and Applications.* Lexington, Mass.: D.C. Heath and Co., 1972.

[13] Eisenbeis, Robert A. "Pitfalls of Discriminant Analysis in Business, Finance, and Economics," *Journal of Finance* 32 (1977): 875–900.

[14] Fama, Eugene F. "Multiperiod Consumption-Investment Decisions," *American Economic Review* 60 (1970): 163–74.

[15] Freund, John E. *Mathmatical Statistics.* Englewood Cliffs, N.J.: Prentice-Hall, 1962.

[16] Fusilier, H. Lee, and Jerome C. Darnell, eds. *Competition and Public Policy: Cases in Antitrust.* Englewood Cliffs, N.J.: Prentice-Hall, 1971.

[17] Gilbert, Ethel S. "On Discrimination Using Qualitative Variables," *Journal of the American Statistical Association* 63 (1968): 1399–1412.

[18] Gilbert, Gary G. "Predicting De Novo Expansion in Bank Merger Cases," *Journal of Finance* 29 (1974): 151–62.

[19] Gilbert, Gary G. "An Analysis of Federal Regulatory Decisions on Market Extension Bank Mergers," *Journal of Money, Credit and Banking* 7 (1975): 81–92.

[20] Glassman, Cynthia A. "Banking Markets in Pennsylvania," Federal Reserve Bank of Philadelphia, 1973.

[21] Goodman, Oscar. "Judical Decisions and Litigation Affecting Competition in Banking," in *Proceedings of a Conference on Bank Structure and Competition.* Federal Reserve Bank of Chicago, 1970.

[22] Green, H.A. John. *Aggregation in Economic Analysis: An Introductory Study.* Princeton, N.J.: Princeton University Press, 1964.

[23] Guttentag, Jack M., and Edward S. Herman. *Banking Structure and Performance.* Bulletin No. 41/43, New York University Graduate School of Business Administration, Institute of Finance, February 1967.

[24] Horowitz, Ira. "Comments on the Ali and Greenbaum Paper," in *Proceedings of a Conference on Bank Structure and Competition.* Federal Reserve Bank of Chicago, 1972.

[25] Horowitz, Ira. "Numbers-Equivalents in United States Manufacturing Industries: 1954, 1958 and 1963," *Southern Economic Journal* 37 (1971): 396–408.

[26] Horvitz, Paul M. "Stimulating Bank Competition Through Regulatory Action," *Journal of Finance* 20 (1965): 1–13.

[27] Johnston, J. *Econometric Methods.* 2nd ed. New York: McGraw-Hill, 1972.

[28] Juncker, George R., and George S. Oldfield. "Projecting Market Structure by Monte Carlo Simulation: A Study of Bank Expansion in New Jersey," *Journal of Finance* 27 (1972): 1101–26.

[29] Kramer, Robert L. "Forecasting Branch Growth Patterns," *Journal of Bank Research* (Winter 1971): 17–24.

[30] Kreps, Clifton H., and Olin S. Pugh. *Money Banking and Monetary Policy*. New York: The Ronald Press Company, 1967.

[31] Miller, Richard A. "Numbers-Equivalents, Relative Entropy, and Concentration Ratios: A Comparison Using Market Performance," *Southern Economic Journal* 39 (1972): 107–12.

[32] Mossin, Jan. "Optimal Multiperiod Portfolio Policies," *Journal of Business* 41 (1968): 215–29.

[33] Mote, Larry R. "A Conceptual Optimal Banking Structure for the United States," in *Proceedings of a Conference on Bank Structure and Competition*. Federal Reserve Bank of Chicago, 1969.

[34] Mullineaux, Donald J. "Branch Versus Unit Banking: An Analysis of Relative Costs," Federal Reserve Bank of Philadelphia, 1973.

[35] Peltzman, Sam. "Bank Stock Prices and the Effects of Regulation of the Banking Structure," *Journal of Business* 41 (1968): 413–30.

[36] Peltzman, Sam. "Entry in Commercial Banking," *The Journal of Law and Economics* VIII (1965): 11–50.

[37] Pennsylvania Banking Law Commission. *Commission's Statement of Issues Involved in Suggestions for Changes in Laws Governing Mergers, Branches, and Holding Companies and Commission's Tentative Conclusions and Reports of Commission's Economic Consultants*. January, 1967.

[38] Phillips, Almarin. "Comments on Mote's Paper," in *Proceedings of a Conference on Bank Structure and Competition*. Federal Reserve Bank of Chicago, 1969.

[39] Phillips, Almarin. "Competition, Confusion, and Commercial Banking," *Journal of Finance* 32 (1964): 32–45.

[40] Piper, Thomas R. *The Economics of Bank Acquisitions by Registered Bank Holding Companies*. Federal Reserve Bank of Boston, 1971.

[41] Sinkey, Joseph F. Jr. "A Multivariate Statistical Analysis of the Characteristics of Problem Banks," *Journal of Finance* 30 (1975): 21–36.

[42] Stuhr, David P. "The Effect of Non-Commercial Bank Competition on Commercial Bank Behavior," (Unpublished Ph.D. Thesis): Graduate School of Business Administration, New York University, 1972.

[43] Theil, H. *Optimal Decision Rules For Government and Industry*. Amsterdam, Netherlands: North-Holland Publishing Company, 1964.

[44] Tobin, James. "Liquidity Preference as Behavior Toward Risk," *Review of Economic Studies* 25 (1958): 65–86.

[45] Yeats, Alexander J. "An Analysis of the Effect of Mergers on the Banking Market Structure," *Journal of Money, Credit and Banking* 5 (1973): 623–36.

Index

Actual competition rule, 46, 98, 116, 125
Acquired bank, 33, 66, 70
Ali, M.M. and S.I. Greenbaum, 120n.
Analysis of variance, 88, 100n.
Autocorrelation, 78
Avery, R.B. and R.A. Eisenbeis, 53n., 54n., 81n.

Bank examination, 11, 60
Bank Holding Company Act of 1956, 38
Bank Merger Act of 1960, 37
Bayes theorem, 84
Bedford market, 115
Behavior categories, 14, 58
Bell, F.W. and N.B. Murphy, 18n., 125n.

California, 11, 13, 31, 34, 35n., 36n.
Central limit theorem, 82
Characteristics
    bank, 10, 18, 26, 29, 33, 58, 68
    market, 39, 58, 75
Cobb-Douglas production function, 8
Cohen, K.J. and S.R. Reid, 81n.
Collinearity, 43
Concentration ratio, 16, 43, 70, 87, 91

Connecticut, 34, 36n.
Contiguous county law, 32, 34, 63, 79, 86, 100, 116
Cooley, W.W. and P.R. Lohnes, 81n.
Cost studies, econometric, 8, 9, 18, 21
Costs
    operating, 8, 9
    transportation, 9

Darnell, J.C. and H.L. Fusilier, 53n.
de novo bank, 10, 12
de novo branching
    behavior, 9, 10, 18, 22, 24, 73, 103
    market, 10, 24, 33
    regulation, 10, 32, 35n., 63, 73
Discriminant analysis, 10, 11, 18, 26, 28, 43, 53n., 123
Distribution, F, 91
District branching law, 34, 35, 63, 86, 96, 116

Econometric cost studies, 8, 9, 18, 21
Economies of scale, 9, 121
Efficiency, 2, 8
Eisenbeis, R.A., 11, 81n.
Eisenbeis, R.A. and R.B. Avery, 53n., 54n., 81n.
Elapsed time accounting, 57, 78

131